John Kavanagh

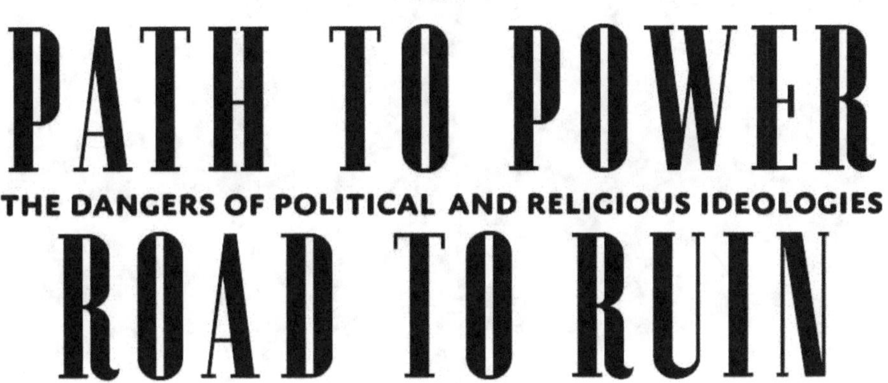

PATH TO POWER

THE DANGERS OF POLITICAL AND RELIGIOUS IDEOLOGIES

ROAD TO RUIN

PATH TO POWER, ROAD TO RUIN

PATH TO POWER, ROAD TO RUIN

For My Wife

John Kavanagh

TABLE OF CONTENTS

Author's Preface   7

CHAPTERS

1. The Promise of Ideology   13

2. The Problem with Ideology   27

3. Ideology Drivers   43

4. Utopianism: Heaven Can Wait   51

5. Absolutism: The Refuge of Small Minds   69

6. Supremacism: Raising Ourselves and Lowering Others   89

7. Three Dangerous Ideas Currently in Play   105

8. The Road to a Better Future   121

Appendix 1: Mass Killing by Ideology   139

Appendix 2: Ideology Definitions   145

Endnotes   149

Bibliography   159

AUTHOR'S PREFACE

I was born into and grew up in a very conservative Irish Catholic family, the son of two immigrants. I was deeply involved in the religious and political ideologies that were taught in my home. I didn't really have any choice. I was compelled to accept the beliefs espoused by my parents, my clergy, and the community in which I lived. I was indoctrinated at a young age and I didn't dare question the ideas presented. Their power over me as an individual was simply overwhelming.

I embraced their beliefs completely, more because of the fear of adult disapproval and the terror of living in excruciating torment in hell for all eternity, than because of their inherent appeal. I realize now, looking back, that I was, for all intents and purposes, a slave to these ideas, oblivious to their true meaning and purpose, and ignorant of their consequences and fallibility. I allowed authority figures of all types to manipulate me and pacify me with their ideologies.

The problem was that my desire for the benefits offered by adherence to their belief systems was strong. The ideologies promised me that my existential anxiety about life and death matters would be substantially reduced, that I would be protected from uncertainty and doubt, and that my status and identity would be raised to new heights. This all anesthetized me to the need to think for myself, to take responsibility for my beliefs, and to accept the challenge of building my own belief structure from the bottom up, rather than embracing ideologies imposed from the top down.

The big issue was that, given my deep emotional and psychological attachment to ideologies, how was I ever going to break free from the bonds of these ideas? The answer was that I wasn't—not without some push from outside of my comfort zone. I needed a trigger, an external event that motivated me to challenge my existing beliefs, to consider alternatives, and to be willing to accept new ideas. Fortunately, over time, my thinking was impacted by two chance events that opened my eyes to the truth about ideologies.

The first trigger was an experience that I had in the confessional at my local Catholic Church when I was a teenager. I went to confess about what would seem to have been a relatively minor infraction. However, the Church deemed it a serious breach of their laws, i.e., eating meat on a Friday. In this specific case, I was served roast beef at a formal dinner, on a Friday night, for young people from the local high schools. Since the meat was the only food option that was made available and the food was being served by a waiter, I made the choice to eat the beef to avoid making a big issue at the dinner table with a dozen other people present. I rationalized it by promising myself that I would eat no meat for the next two days, a commitment which I kept.

But the next day, feeling badly about my decision, I went to church and confessed my sin to the local priest. His response was to tell me that I had committed a mortal sin, and that if I had died in a car accident after the dinner, I would have gone straight to hell. Because I knew my catechism, was so invested in my beliefs, and was so deeply in the sway of the important adults in my life, I accepted the Priest's judgment and moved on. But I never forgot the experience.

Under normal circumstances, that would have been the end of the matter. But, as fate would have it, several years later, when I was driving to visit a friend at a nearby college, I heard on the radio that the Roman Catholic Church hierarchy in Rome had decided that Catholics would no longer go to hell for eating meat on Friday. The effect this news had on me was stunning. My immediate reaction was: What happened to all the Catholics who had spent centuries suffering eternal torment in hell for eating meat on Friday? I felt that, at a minimum, they had experienced a tremendous injustice at the hands of God or his Church; or at the maximum, they had experienced excruciating eternal torment that was completely unnecessary. Either way, it seemed as if the Church was deliberately using fear and terror tactics to compel unquestioning obedience to Church laws, no matter how unimportant.

The second thought I had was that, if the consequences of violating one of the Church's laws--one that had been in place for over eleven hundred years--could be reversed so easily, how could any church law have any validity at all? For me, the answer was that Church laws were just that, Church laws. They were not God's laws, because God would not make the mistake of punishing people unjustly. Instead, I was inclined to conclude that Church laws were merely constructs of men and therefore very fallible. I did not have to obey Church law, just God's law.

For the first time in my life, I had a reason to challenge the fundamental validity of my childhood religious beliefs. I began thinking differently about the Catholic Church. I was no longer so in awe of the Church. I started to spend a good deal of my spare time studying all the major religions and reading their sacred texts to learn more about their fundamental tenets and doctrines. I wanted to see if any of them offered me a better alternative. Unfortunately, none really did. There was, in my view, a surprising sameness to all of them.

For a while, that was as far as my search went. I kept on going to a Christian church; I continued to accept the same broad principles that I had always held; and I brought my children up to believe the same things. I just could not let go of my religious beliefs. They were like an addiction, holding the same power over me as a narcotic would, in spite of their obvious flaws and dangers. It was clear that it would take a much more powerful trigger to motivate me to effect a significant change in my ideological proclivities.

The second trigger occurred several years later during a chance visit to the Yale College Bookstore in New Haven, Connecticut. On this trip, I came across what was, for me, a truly astonishing book. It was co-edited by a Yale professor, Ben Kiernan, and his colleague, Robert Gellately, and was entitled, *The Specter of Genocide, Mass Murder in Historical Perspective.* Reading it was shocking, because in spite of my "sophisticated" education, I realized that I was really under-informed and quite naïve about human beliefs and behavior.

I knew I had to do something about this deficiency and began reading Kiernan's other books on the subject, as well as numerous books by other authors that offered detailed descriptions and explanations for the mass murders highlighted in *The Specter of Genocide.* These books showed me a view of life that I almost could not comprehend.

First, they demonstrated that the mass slaughter of humans has been a surprisingly frequent occurrence throughout history—there have been over one hundred instances in history where one hundred thousand or more people were killed.[1] Second, they showed that the killings and all that surrounded them unleashed a savagery, a degree of human brutality, and an amount of human suffering that was almost unimaginable. Third, they indicated that all peoples in all areas of the world had been participants in these atrocities at one time or another. And fourth, they made it obvious that a handful of history's most pervasive ideologies had played an important role in the majority of the large scale killing incidents, either triggering, sustaining, rationalizing, or justifying these horrific actions.

Ideologies' complicity in these horrific events and the extensive human suffering involved were the two most disturbing findings to come out of my research. Given that I had been so heavily invested in my own versions of these religious and political ideologies for so long, and given that I had naively thought that these beliefs were beneficial for mankind, I found the four lessons learned quite upsetting. They raised a lot of questions for me.

How could I have been blind to the flaws of the ideologies that were so much a part of my life? How could I have been so unaware of the incalculable suffering people had experienced at the hands of leading ideologies? How could I not have seen the need to think though the implications and consequences of my beliefs? And how, given what I had learned about the Catholic Church years earlier, had I not realized a long time ago that my continuing commitment to these types of beliefs was unsustainable?

I felt, given my own failure to address these issues throughout my life, that it was time for me, now that I was retired, to make an effort to get answers to the questions I posed. This led me to embark on a serious and extensive program of study of ideologies and belief systems. In the process, I went on to read over one hundred books and dozens of journal articles that analyzed mass killing case histories, that defined the pros and cons of the religious and political belief systems involved, that spelled out and analyzed the sacred texts of leading religions, that described ideologies and the leaders that exploited them, that defined the outcomes of implementing ideologies in history, that studied the evolution of ideologies and their drivers, that provided alternatives to ideologies and ideological thinking, and that assessed the effectiveness of human thinking processes as they relate to belief formation.

This research was then distilled and became the basis for the views articulated in this book. What I learned from my analysis was quite different from what I had expected when I began the project. It turned out that the costs of embracing ideologies and ideological thinking were much worse than I expected, so much so that I was motivated to share the results with other people. I wanted to help people understand what they are committing to when they accept ideologies without proper consideration.

I wrote this book to appeal to a mainstream audience, not an academic audience. I am focused on helping ordinary people, like myself, who are bound to old ideas that don't make sense any more, but who are unable to escape to a new and better, more objective reality. I know, from personal experience, that it is not easy to end our dependence on ideologies. But, it is something we all must do. We have to stand up for ourselves, rejecting ideologies imposed on us from on high in favor of defining our own beliefs and our own destiny.

The result is definitely worth the effort. Holding beliefs, based on objective reality rather than on faith, myths, or the manipulations of others, does in fact lead to superior outcomes. In the last chapter of this book, I show how the more analytic, fact-based approach has helped many people in all walks of life--including business, investments, sports, military conflict, and psychotherapy—outperform their peers. The difference in results is quite surprising.

I believe we all would benefit tremendously from facing the reality of our lives, taking full responsibility for our situations, making a thorough investigation of our beliefs, and then changing them accordingly. We need to be able to say: "I don't have to be afraid," "I don't have to think what other people think," "I can think for myself," "I can break away and form my own destiny."

Personally, I am a much happier and better person for having made the effort to develop a more accurate view of the world and change my perspective about what is true and what is not. I hope this book can assist you in your efforts to do the same.

Chapter 1

THE PROMISE OF IDEOLOGY

Throughout history, smart, ambitious people have realized that, if they wanted to acquire power, dominate their societies, accumulate wealth, and bring about significant change, they had to find effective ways to attract, influence, manipulate, and control large numbers of people. They learned, from experience, that one of the best ways to do this was to harness the motivational and organizational power of mankind's belief systems and to use that clout to persuade people to join their group, commit to their causes, and support their societal agendas.

Prospective leaders seeking power, existing bosses trying to hold onto and expand their base of control, and wealthy people trying to manipulate the system in their favor have long understood the power of ideologies and exploited them ruthlessly. These elites use ideologies because they are well-organized systems of beliefs that can serve as the basis for developing, implementing, and rationalizing religious, political, and social programs. They have special value because they are narratives, elaborate stories, that can gain people's interest, link multiple beliefs and ideas into comprehensive views of the world, change minds, and present a roadmap for ordinary people to follow.

There are scores of different ideologies, each with its own unique interpretation of the world and each with its own special vision of how a particular group of people can best progress going forward. These more sophisticated versions have typically been composed of several core elements, including:

- A story about how and why society has evolved over time to its current state;
- A statement of the issues that need to be resolved if society is to advance to a new stage of development;

- A description of the values, beliefs, and practices that should regulate society in the future;

- A set of goals and action plans that would advance its progress going forward;

- A delineation of why the proposed belief system is better than the existing or previous belief systems; and

- A specification of the authority that supposedly legitimizes the ideology and gives followers the permission to wholeheartedly embrace its beliefs.

Typically, these six elements have been woven together into packages of beliefs that have created compelling narrative stories that motivate people to buy into the ideas presented by the leaders who exploit the ideologies.

These structured belief systems have been uniquely persuasive because their creeds and doctrines have offered potential adherents benefits they desperately wanted and needed, i.e., the promise of a better life or better world, the lessening of fear and existential anxiety, the elimination of doubt and uncertainty, a chance to feel special and better than others, or an opportunity to be involved in a cause or group that could give meaning to their lives. By building such strong links to human wishes, desires, longings, and fears, mankind's ideologies have become one of the most influential, powerful, and pervasive forms of human thought ever created.

These belief systems have often been created by an individual or individuals who claimed they had a special insight into the functioning of the world and how it could be made better. These "founders" came from all walks of life. Some were prophets, like Jesus and Mohammed; others were political economists, like Marx and Engels; still others were political theorists, like Lenin and Mao; and many were politicians, like Adolf Hitler and Benito Mussolini. Their ideas leveraged a variety of sources. Religions, like Islam, Christianity, and Judaism depended on divine revelation codified in sacred texts; communism exploited political and economic analysis; racism relied on sociological and biological study, and National Socialism on historical analysis.

The initial beliefs of the founders were usually co-opted and developed into more comprehensive frameworks by people who came along afterwards. For instance, Lenin, Trotsky, Stalin and other leaders of the Russian Revolution built on the theories of communism put forward by Marx and Engels. Similarly, the leaders of the early Catholic Church leveraged the teachings of Jesus, Paul, and the Apostles to create a hard set of fixed principles that was codified by Church Councils in the fourth century CE.

Then, in each case, those who followed created the institutions and hierarchy needed to ensure that the ideology would be perpetuated. Because many of these ideologies evolved over a long period of time and were thoroughly evaluated and debated, their doctrines easily became fixed and dogmatic, typically consisting of hard and fast rules that were non-negotiable and could not be subjected to any challenge or modification. They were presented as an integrated package and had to be accepted as such.

Deviation from and questioning of core principles was not allowed because the founders and adherents believed that their doctrine was an ultimate truth, surpassing all others. As a result, ideologies often became an all-encompassing reality, eliminating all alternative views, and actively discouraging individuals from carefully thinking about their beliefs. Everyone who participated in the belief system was asked to see the world through the filter of the ideological principles enunciated by the leaders.

While time consuming development processes were typical for belief systems in the past, new ideological narratives take much less time to be created and disseminated. First, they are not brand new ideas that need lengthy maturation. Instead, they are generally extensions of old belief systems that have existed for centuries, but have now been repurposed or repositioned to reflect modern realities. Second, they have the benefit of coming to market in an era when the process of spreading ideas has been significantly accelerated through the sophisticated use of modern communication and marketing technologies. Third, they are often created/disseminated within the confines of an authoritarian or totalitarian system where ideologies are dictated under threat of violence. So, there is no longer an extended process of conversion over decades or centuries. An entire population can be compelled to accept a belief system quickly, in days and years.

Today's leaders are making aggressive use of these reimagined ideologies, especially their more dogmatic versions, to gain control of us and help sell and justify their national agenda and programs. Their ideas are readily accepted because most people are very uncritical in their evaluation of these appeals, are easily seduced into accepting them, have little basis or information to critique them, or may be forced to comply because of the threat of death or imprisonment. As a result, these updated ideology versions spread rapidly and become a serious threat to human freedom and societal advancement. Distressingly, there are many current examples of this phenomenon.

Vladimir Putin, the President of Russia, is trying to build a new Russian Empire. He is attempting to recapture what he perceives to be the lost glory from the Soviet era, when Russia's armies drove the Nazi invaders from the country, annexed all of Eastern Europe, and then stood toe-to-toe with the United States for forty years. As part of this imperial initiative, he has ordered the invasion and systematic destruction of Ukraine. The invasion has already cost hundreds of thousands of lives, done inestimable damage to the Ukrainian economy and infrastructure, forced millions of people to flee to neighboring countries, and subjected Ukrainians to vicious brutality and often war crimes.

Putin justified his actions and the substantial harm being inflicted on the Ukrainian people by creating and disseminating an ideologically slanted, five thousand word position paper called, *On The Historical Unity of Russians and Ukrainians.*[1] His essay spells out his reasons for invading Ukraine. He uses an imperialist narrative, with religious and nationalistic arguments, as a tool to justify his illegitimate actions to his own people, to Russia's allies/potential allies, and to the rest of the outside world. He has distributed it broadly and repetitively to his national media, to the internet, to his leadership, the military, and even to schools. And finally, he went one step further and codified his views into law.

Putin claims that, among other things, that Ukraine lies within Russia's historical borders, that it has been part of Russia for over one thousand years, that Russia and Ukraine share a common history, culture, religion, and language and should, therefore, be one country. He further asserts that the West has been undermining Russia's historic position in Ukraine by fomenting dissent, by encouraging revolution, and by installing leaders who are antagonistic to Russia (and planning to ally with the West).

He goes on to say that the fall of the Soviet Union was a catastrophe that was engineered by the West. When combined with the aggressive eastward growth of NATO to include many of the old Soviet Bloc countries, it has created an untenable situation for Russia. Given that

                                              PATH TO POWER, ROAD TO RUIN

Putin, and now his people, believe that his country deserves great power status and is being threatened by the continuing expansion of NATO, he asserts that Russia was entitled to a much larger sphere of influence/domination that would include Eastern Europe. This notion holds great appeal for his people who want to believe that they deserve to be a great country again, like they were after they defeated the Nazis in 1945.

Since the West has consistently been unwilling to respect Russia's claims and negotiate an accommodation with Russia, Putin suggested he would take matters into his own hands and invade Ukraine to prevent it from becoming part of NATO. He claimed that the matter required great urgency because he asserted that Russian speaking people in Ukraine were being threatened. He also declared that Nazis and gays were inserting themselves into the country and undermining the morality of the people as dictated by the Russian Orthodox Church.

The Ukrainian leadership and people and their allies in the West have forcefully disagreed with Putin's narrative. They believe Ukraine deserves to remain an independent country. Contrary to Putin's narrative, the Ukrainians did not welcome the Russians with open arms when they invaded in February of 2022. Their country was not overrun with Nazis and gays. Instead, they have vigorously and successfully defended their territory against the Russian aggression and have actively sought and received the help of the West to preserve their nationhood and democracy.

Putin's need to distract his people from his inadequacies as a leader and his personal desire to go down in history as a great conqueror of other nations does not justify his illegal actions. His narrative is false; and his use of this false narrative against the interests of his people is cynical and dangerous.

Sadly, Putin is not alone in using this approach to control his people and the agenda of his nation. Xi Jinping, the President of the People's Republic of China, has embarked on a decades-long program to return China to its former greatness, to make its people proud of their nation, and to motivate them to make great sacrifices. The purpose: to enable China to take its deserved place as the pre-eminent country in the world. In short, as Xi has said, on many occasions, China has the right to pursue its legitimate interests and its stated goal of achieving *The Great Rejuvenation of the Chinese Nation.*

This initiative will allow him to rationalize the complete subjugation of his own people, the incredibly rapid expansion of his military capabilities, and his clear intent to have China become the dominant power in the world.

According to Xi, China is a 5000 year old civilization, a great nation with a glorious past. Xi claims that, at one time, it was the center of the known world and a country that dominated east Asia, so much so that all surrounding countries paid homage to its emperor as vassal states. Inevitably, as most great nations do, China suffered a period of significant stagnation and decline in the 19th century. Western powers and the Japanese exploited this moment of weakness and invaded China. They stole the resources of the country, marginalized and brutalized its people, and took over its governance.

Xi's narrative goes on to say that the Chinese Communist Party, under the leadership of Mao-Zedong, drove all China's enemies, including the Japanese, out of China. In 1949, China began the long process of re-establishing itself as a major player on the world stage. Over the roughly seventy-five years since the communists seized control, the country has advanced steadily to become a leading technological, economic, political, and military power in the world.

Through its Belt and Road program, its Asia Development Bank, its Asia Infrastructure Bank, and its holding key positions in major global organizations, like the World Health Organization and the United Nations, the country's influence is spreading worldwide. China is on its way to becoming a superpower and restoring its position of supremacy among all nations. In pursuit of that goal, China will stop at nothing and will not allow anyone to interfere with its advancing its so-called legitimate interests. China's ultimate ambition is to overthrow the current liberal democratic world order and replace it with a new world order with China as the head.

China's grand vision is disseminated to the Chinese people in all its communications—on State TV, in the State media, on the government-controlled internet, in its schools, and in all the publications and speeches of its leaders. The message is also spread through its extensive disinformation campaigns, its media stations around the world, its Confucius Institutes, and through its cadres positioned throughout Chinese society. Its purpose is to excite and distract its people, to make them feel great pride in their nation, to make them believe that the Chinese Communist Party is the font of all China's great accomplishments and is, therefore, indispensable to the nation. By giving people pride and the chance to be rich and live a comfortable lifestyle, the

                                    PATH TO POWER, ROAD TO RUIN

Chinese leadership is merely pacifying its people, keeping them in a drug-like stupor while they pursue their relentless effort to create the ultimate totalitarian project in China, rivaling George Orwell's *1984*.

This ideological positioning allows the leaders to proceed with the expansion of a totalitarian regime that represses and controls the Chinese people to an extent never seen in world history. China has eliminated all alternative belief systems--having driven three religions, the Falun Gong, Tibetan Buddhism, and Islam virtually out of existence. It exercises total censorship over any ideas that do not fit with Party propaganda. All internal opposition is eliminated through purges, violence, corruption trials, and a huge state security system that is supported by advanced surveillance technology. All external opposition from outside China has been neutralized by using economic leverage and bullying to get Chinese geopolitical positions accepted around the world. In the long run, China will use its extensive and rapidly growing military capability as a blunt instrument of dominion and control.

The problem with the wonderful story presented by Chinese leadership is that it is not entirely true; and it definitely overlooks a great deal of what has happened over the course of Chinese history. China has not been a single unified entity throughout its entire history. It has had golden ages and periods of stability, but it also has been riven by civil wars, in which regional warlords or competing ideologies have battled each other for control of its territory. Furthermore, it has been conquered by outsiders at several times…yes, the European powers and Japan in the 19th and 20th centuries, but also the Mongols in the 13th century and the Manchu in the 17th century, each of whom killed tens of millions of Chinese during their conquests of all or parts of the country.

Xi's China narrative also overlooks the reality that, over the past several centuries, there have been many violent and bloody revolutions against the reigning Chinese authority, including the Taiping, Panthay, and Dzungar rebellions. Tens of millions have died. Further, during the period when Chairman Mao ruled the country, from 1949 to 1976, as many as forty million people died as a result of Mao's failed policies, including Mao's Great Famine, the Great Proletarian Cultural Revolution, and the Invasion of Tibet.

Xi's version of Chinese history and greatness is in need of revision. Nonetheless, it has gained traction with the Chinese people; and this, in turn, has allowed its leadership to proceed with its ambitious and repressive mission.

Unfortunately, it is not just dictators, like Xi and Putin, who are using ideologies to restructure their countries along totalitarian lines, taking away all freedoms, undermining the rule of law, crushing any dissent, and arbitrarily seizing whatever they want to enrich themselves. We, in America, are headed down the same path. Trump and the ideological right are selling the citizens of our country a set of ideas that are designed to radically change the fundamental structure of our government and American democracy. Their philosophy encompasses several dangerous streams of thought, each of which is itself an independent ideology in its own right. Taken together, they represent a seductive belief system that has captured the minds of millions and threatens to subvert two hundred and fifty years of democracy. These ideas include three reactionary belief systems, including Christian nationalism (discussed in this chapter), libertarianism (discussed in this chapter), and white male supremacism (discussed in Chapter 6), all positioned under the "Make America Great Again" umbrella.

The first, and in some ways, most important of these three ideological strains is Christian nationalism. In the United States, Christian nationalism has moved from the fringe to the mainstream as the result of aggressive efforts by very well-funded and powerful individuals and interest groups. They want to push America from a democracy to an autocracy, so their ideological positions can become the dominant narrative and they can eliminate all alternative views from our society's dialogue.

The rise of Christian nationalism reflects some important shifts in Americans attitudes towards Christianity specifically and religion in general. Pew Research studies demonstrate that the number of people in the United States who claim they are Christian has been declining steadily over the last several decades, from 90% in 1972 to 63% in 2021.[2] As a result, many Christians feel that their existence and status in society is being threatened and that they need to take action to restore their dominant standing.

There is an ever expanding number of Christians in the United States who are espousing more radical views of the importance and role of Christianity in our society. They claim that America was established as a Christian nation, that our founders were themselves Christian, and that our founding documents, the Constitution and the Declaration of Independence, were based on Judeo-Christian principles, or, more narrowly, the Bible. They believe that these realities entitle them to forcefully reassert their privileged status in society.

Christian Nationalists seek to rewrite history, re-establish white, Christian, male supremacy in America, and to marginalize women, minorities, the non-religious, and members of other religions. But, in reality, their ultimate goal is to create a theocratic dictatorship, run according to Biblical law and a fundamentalist interpretation of scripture. They want to push Christian religious beliefs into all corners of American society, much as communism was inserted into all of Russia and radical Islam was inserted into Saudi Arabia years ago. Their idea would be to eliminate any line of thought that is inconsistent with the teachings of the Christian church and to use the United States government's revenue to inculcate conservative Christian principles throughout the country. Christian Nationalists' hope to merge American and Christian identities, so that being Christian is a fundamental part of being American.

If Christian Nationalists behave like those who run Muslim theocracies—and they inevitably will, then patriarchy will reign and women's place will be in the home having babies. Non-Christians, non-whites, and immigrants will be considered second class citizens and may be excluded from the full privileges of the society. Abortion would be outlawed nationally and contraceptives will likely be banned so the US could grow the white Christian population and make the country predominantly white once again.

Christian Nationalists would support teaching the Bible in public schools, inserting Christianity into textbooks, eliminating any literature deemed offensive from reading lists, rejecting evolution and climate science, de-emphasizing science and math in school curricula, and limiting female education. Importantly, they would restrict the ability of the media, academia, or government to contradict or undermine the positions taken by religious institutions in the United States.

These actions would effectively represent a return to the Middle Ages when the Catholic Church completely and violently dominated European Society. We all know that this period of history was disastrous for humanity. It created a corrupt and repressive totalitarian society that stultified human progress and development, much as Islamic theocracies have in the Middle East.

And Christian Nationalists today are just as autocratic as they were a thousand years ago. In a recent Public Religion Research Institute/ Brooking survey, "half of Christian nationalism adherents and 40% of sympathizers would support the idea of an authoritarian leader in order to keep Christian values in society."[3]

Further, if you compare the teachings of the Bible to the principles spelled out in the Constitution, you can easily see that religion's rules are definitively anti-democratic and in stark conflict to the principles enshrined in the Constitution. Andrew Seidel, the author of the book, *The Founding Myth,*[4] makes the following points in support of this idea:

The Bible clearly indicates that any attempt to overthrow the established order would not be allowed because God has said that it was He who had chosen earthly rulers; and his people must obey them. Otherwise, they would be sinning against God. If this stricture had held in 18th Century America, there would have been no American Revolution and no Constitution.

In Christianity, there is a presumption of guilt. In witch trials and during the Inquisition, all accused were presumed guilty. If someone was charged, it was assumed that they would be found guilty, just as they are in the court systems in Russia or China today. Under the Constitution, people are innocent until proven guilty by a jury of their peers in a court room, where objectively determined evidence is presented and weighed.

In the Bible, Jesus tells us that we can be punished for our thoughts as well as our actions. According to the First Amendment, we are free to think whatever we want without sanction. We cannot be punished for our thoughts, only our actions.

In the Bible, we could only commit crimes against our fellow believers, not against outsiders. So the law, as described in the Bible, only applied to a select few. The Constitution, on the other hand, states that American laws apply equally to everyone, regardless of race, creed, color, or group affiliation.

The Constitution makes it clear that, in the United States, people are responsible only for their own sins. In America, no one can be punished for the sins of others. Not so in the Bible, where all mankind bears the responsibility for the Original Sin of Adam and Eve.

The Bible provides a justification for slavery and asserts that slaves and women were of lower status than men. The Constitution was amended to eliminate slavery and make women equal to men before the law.

Finally, it is obvious, from reading the Constitution, that it specifically rejects mixing religion and government. The word God never appears in the Constitution. There is no call for divine intervention or indication of divine inspiration as many Christians claim. The three words that open the Constitution, "We The People," indicate that its force emanates from the people not from religion.[5]

Further, the First Amendment to the Constitution spells out four principles that have served America well for almost two hundred and fifty years and that demonstrate that claims of Christian Nationalists are without substance. Those principles are: "people of all faiths and none have the right and responsibility to engage constructively in the public square;" "one's religious affiliation, or lack thereof, should be irrelevant to one's standing in the civic community;" "government should not prefer one religion over another or religion over non-religion;" and "religious instruction is best left to our worship and other religious institutions."[6]

In addition to Christian Nationalism, there is yet another disruptive ideology, libertarianism, that is gaining influence and power in the United States today. A group of very wealthy families, business leaders, and their allies in the Republican Party, are aggressively trying to promote a libertarian ideology. This emerging belief system seeks to undermine the rule of law, the US government that enforces it, and important societal initiatives that are essential for the country's future.

At the level of an individual, libertarianism is the desire to have no limits on individual freedom and choice, e.g., no mask mandates, no vaccine mandates, no restrictions on gun ownership/use, and no health care mandates, regardless of the consequences for the rest of society. At the societal or corporate level, it means an economy unhindered by any restraint, any regulation, any restrictive laws, any punishments for bad or anti-social corporate behavior and the complete elimination of all programs that increase government size and spending, which require higher levels of taxation.

Libertarians strongly favor unrestrained free markets and economic policies that are geared to maximizing growth and profitability at the expense of all other goals. Libertarians would like to substantially reduce or eliminate corporate and personal taxes and IRS enforcement of the payment of those taxes by cutting audit and compliance staff. They would slash government expenditures substantially, whether that be cutting or eliminating social services like Social Security, Medicare, and Medicaid, or significantly shrinking the US military budget by reducing our military's force posture around the world and withdrawing from all commitments and alliances. Further, they would eliminate all regulatory agencies and regulation, especially those involved in environmental areas, such as restrictions on dumping chemicals, pollutants, and noxious gases into the environment. At its heart, libertarianism is essentially an effort to substantially defund or eliminate the government of the United States.

Libertarians oppose any large-scale, government-sponsored programs, like national healthcare or climate initiatives, that could result in significant increases in government spending and bureaucracy and that would have to be funded by increased taxation. For example, in the climate area, they have spent enormous sums to discredit climate science by saying that the science of climate change is unsettled and that there is no proof of global warming. They take this position even though there is near unanimous assent among scientists that climate change is happening and is caused/aggravated by humans.

According to Jane Mayer, in her book *Dark Money*[7] very wealthy libertarians have been exceptionally aggressive in promoting these ideas. They have engaged in well-funded campaigns, spending hundreds of millions and even billions of dollars, to reposition their ideology to make it seem acceptable to a mainstream audience. Their goal is to promote their own views at the expense of others, to have their views widely accepted, and to eventually be dominant. They do this by stealth. They do not submit their positions to be analyzed in the public marketplace for ideas. Instead, they seek to get them entrenched without people being aware of the changes that are actually happening. They push the ideas, not because they believe they are true, but because they want to remove government from their lives and be able to continue to operate without interference and or restraint.

They do this in a variety of ways. They aggressively fund a wide variety of think tanks that have fellows that support their libertarian positions. They use these influencers to put together position papers that support their views with persuasive, but highly misleading language and inadequate substantiation. They lobby Congress aggressively. They control state and local legislatures, which allows them to pass laws in support of their positions so their views can be institutionalized. They have media personalities and celebrities endorse them and their ideas. They create academic programs that tout these ideas and get them taught in schools. They use advocacy and grass roots campaigns to spread their ideas. In pursuit of their goal of spreading their ideology, anything is permitted, including making false claims with regard to the impact of their beliefs. Since most people do not think critically or analyze their positions, they pass as the truth.

When objectively analyzed, it is questionable that such a

libertarian view of civil society is beneficial. The reality is that if everyone in the country doesn't pull together to achieve society's goals, we will inevitably fail. While it is true that we don't want to overburden the economy with excessive regulation and costs, we do need the protections of government to keep the unrestrained power of large corporations and ultra-wealthy people in check. We want to make certain that ordinary citizens are protected from bad actors who wantonly pollute the environment with toxic chemicals, who exploit workers with poor pay and poor working conditions, who steal from society, and whose primary goal in life is the aggrandizement of wealth and power.

It is clear from a review of what Putin, Xi, Christian Nationalists, and Libertarians are proposing, that these belief systems all have a great deal in common in spite of their doctrinal differences. They all want to restructure their societies according their own particular vision of the world or their own private self-interest. They construct and aggressively market dishonest narratives to sell their points of view or rationalize the actions they are taking and the plans they are implementing. And all show a disturbing tendency to rewrite history and push society toward totalitarianism or a plutocratic form of government, in which a small group of very wealthy people rule the country.

Each of these four ideologically-based strategies can lead to dire outcomes for the entire world and pose a serious threat to our country and our democracy. They garner support by exploiting people's fears and making them think they are being persecuted and constrained by outside forces. They each tell their constituencies that they have own particular enemy that keeps their country from realizing its full potential. For Russia, it is the West and NATO; for China it is the United States and members of the liberal world order; for Christian nationalists it is non-Christians and secularists that are to blame; and for libertarians it is the U.S. government, the IRS, and the "Deep State." To defeat their respective enemies, they are individually and collectively spending billions to sell their narratives to their publics or target audiences; and they are using multiple media to disseminate their views broadly in order to dominate the airwaves and drown out and discredit all other views.

As we can clearly see, these four ideologies--and others like them, including Muslim extremism in the Middle East and Hindu Nationalism in India--are growing in influence and power, as more and more people accept them. Leaders' presentations of these ideas are designed to seduce us into accepting their worldview so that we will ignore their real motives for selling us their ideologies. They all ultimately seek to structure society along ideological lines; and they are all set up to enhance the position of powerful and very wealthy elites. In doing so, they will ultimately or have already eliminated democracy in their societies.

We have to recognize that the leaders' ideological visions are like drugs. They anesthetize us to the reality of what they are doing. We buy in because we all want the high of thinking that ours will be a great nation, that we will prevail against our enemies, that there will be a utopian outcome to our lives, or that there will be some God or strongman who will take care of us. So we accept the leaders' belief systems, not recognizing that we have had and will continue to have to pay a very high price for acquiescing to their views.

Chapter 2

THE PROBLEM WITH IDEOLOGY

Blind acceptance of and commitment to religious and political ideologies has caused an enormous amount of human suffering. The problem is that when we whole-heartedly embrace an ideological belief framework, we tend to buy in to all of it and forego thinking it through carefully. We accept many assumptions made by others, without thorough examination, and don't ask for proof of the many claims made. We become blind to reality and embrace false premises about the world around us and the people with whom we have to interact.

This is especially true when an idea exploits the pre-existing beliefs, commitments, and prejudices that we all develop and cling to in our lives. This disables our critical faculties and causes us to buy into hatred and demonization of others, to promises about the future that can never be fulfilled, and to ideas that foreclose alternatives that might lead to constructive change.

When this acquiescence occurs, leaders who are pursuing power and wealth can manipulate us in significant ways. We have no defense against their sales pitch and become ultra-loyal to them because they appear to speak directly to our needs and biases. When they get control of our minds, leaders end up having few, if any, restraints on their actions and become accountable only to themselves. We give them a blank check. This allows leaders to proceed with forcibly eliminating all opposition to their will or their belief agenda and programs.

Most people in society aren't going to object. They aren't going to put themselves at risk. They aren't going to sacrifice their lives or put their families at risk for some vague social objective. So, in these situations, the leaders get bolder because they have nothing to restrain them and, as a result, their actions become more and more severe. Many times they will pursue their goals all the way to the worst possible outcome. This tendency has led to ideologies generating very bad results for humanity.

The destructive effects of human belief systems have typically manifested themselves in several different ways. They have triggered brutal mass killing events; they have severely exacerbated and prolonged major human conflicts; they have blocked mankind's efforts to coalesce around solutions to some of humanity's most pressing problems; they have constrained society to such an extent that they have retarded human progress; they have polarized people into irreconcilable groups that paralyze their societies; and they have justified brutal repression and exploitation of select groups of people. In each of these situations, ideologies and ideological conflict have led to extreme outcomes and significant human suffering.

The most significant and most deadly consequence of accepting ideological thinking has been its tendency to drive the mass killing of humans. It is simply astonishing how many times extraordinarily large numbers of people have been targeted and systematically killed in the name of their beliefs or those of other people.

Today, most people are aware of only a few high-profile instances of ideologically-driven mass murder, such as the Holocaust, the Killing Fields in Cambodia, and the slaughter of Tutsis in Rwanda. However, they generally do not realize that they are just scratching the surface on this issue. The reality is that there have been over one hundred known occasions where one hundred thousand or more people have been murdered at one time and place, and, in half of those cases, the death toll was in excess of one million people per incident.[1] As significant as these specific occurrences are, they only constitute a fraction of the deaths from mass killing. As many as four to five hundred million people have been murdered over time in this way.[2] Such numbers are almost impossible to fathom. But, they are a reality of human history. And it appears that many of these killings have been ideologically-motivated.

The most egregious instances of this murderous behavior can be linked to several of history's most pervasive ideologies—Imperialism, Communism, Nationalism, Racism, Islam, and Christianity. (See Appendix 1 for details, by ideology, for each major killing incident, the triggering event, and the number killed; and then see Appendix 2 on what is, and is not, considered an ideology.)

Of the six belief systems listed above, imperialism has been the most deadly killer, at over two hundred millions deaths worldwide. Imperialism kills because it is a set of ideas that is both an impetus to and a justification of a nation's drive to create an empire and dominate others through military, economic, and political power. Imperialistic attitudes and ideologies give leaders and countries with expansionist ambitions the rationale that makes it acceptable for them to seize the lands of defeated populations, to steal their money and possessions, to impose taxes on them, to exploit their natural resources, to create living space for favored groups in their home country, and to raise money by selling conquered peoples into slavery.

Imperialists rationalize their behavior in two ways. Either they cite contrived historical analyses, such as the Putin's aforementioned essay, *The Historical Unity of Russians and Ukrainians*; or they claim that their technical, cultural, and military preeminence over their targeted populations demonstrates their inherent superiority, which in turn justifies their taking any action needed to bring more primitive people up to their level.

Imperialistic programs have historically been especially violent because they have had, of necessity, to involve military conquest and the forcible eradication of resistance to invasion and occupation. The inevitable result has been the mass killing of soldiers and civilians as well as the propagation of fear and terror, all to ensure the complete submission of conquered peoples to the imperialist forces and their continuing obedience to their colonial rule.

Some of the worst mass slaughters in history have been imperialistically inspired. The Mongols' invasion westward from Asia to Europe and Africa, the Manchu conquest of China, Tamerlane's predations, European imperialists actions in the Americas and Africa, and Imperial Japan and Nazi Germany's invasions of countries in Asia and Europe are all prime examples of this phenomenon.[3]

Communist regimes were the second most aggressive drivers of mass murder after imperialists, killing almost one hundred million people. The process of bringing about communist revolutions, establishing viable communist states, and radically restructuring societies caused unparalleled human suffering and death. Mass killing seems to have been the inevitable outcome of all attempts to implement and sustain communist ideologies. This devastating end result has occurred because all communist revolutions had a dual mandate to essentially do the impossible, i.e., both to create a new "ideal" society and also to bring about a new and better mankind.

Communist leaders believed that the achievement of these far-reaching goals necessitated a complete restructuring of society, including the elimination of the upper classes, the redistribution of their property, the nationalization of industry, the collectivization of agriculture, and the elevation of the working classes to the top rung of society. Given the radical and rapid transformation required to accomplish these sweeping changes, there was inevitably going to be a violent struggle between those who wanted to revolutionize the social order and those who wanted to cling to the old structures.

For communist leaders, there could be no compromise, no negotiation, and no temporizing with those who were unwilling to accept the transformation to communism. People who thought in the old way, who resisted necessary change, who wanted to protect and defend what they had, and who appeared to be blocking progress toward the creation of a new socialist state had to be swept away. Terror, purposeful mass starvation, vast slave labor projects, and totalitarian rule, enforced by the military, the secret police, and an extensive prison system, were deemed essential to bring about the kind of societal overhaul and economic modernization required to make communism work. In the process, communist regimes in Russia, China, Cambodia, North Korea, Vietnam, and several African countries, were responsible for the deaths of tens of millions of their own citizens.[4]

Nationalism has been the third most significant driver of mass murder, after imperialism and communism. Nationalism is commonly described as "a sense of national consciousness, exalting one nation above all others, and placing primary emphasis on the promotion of its culture and interests, as opposed to those of other nations or supranational groups."[5]

Politicians, demagogues and other erstwhile leaders seeking power frequently use nationalistic appeals to garner support for their political agenda because such messages build their followers' self-esteem and play to their prejudice against foreigners. Such messaging helps motivate people to work toward important national goals, making nationalism appear, on the surface, to be a very positive force for any society. However, nationalism can and does become dangerous in two circumstances:

The first occurs when pursuit of a national vision becomes so single-minded that it fails to consider the consequences for all peoples. For example, America's dream of Manifest Destiny and coast-to-coast expansion was realized at the expense of millions of Native Americans,

                                          PATH TO POWER, ROAD TO RUIN

who were driven from their lands, exposed to fatal diseases, and killed off by white settlers and the military.[6]

The second occurs when a nation has been humiliated by its own failures, the loss of its empire, or its subjugation by others. These experiences can act as catalyzing agents for the implementation of programs designed to return that nation to its former greatness and to restore the dignity of its people. In the twentieth century, four nations-- Imperial Japan, Nazi Germany, Ottoman Turkey, Khmer Rouge Cambodia—followed this path to most devastating effect, leading to a world war and several genocides. Again millions of people died as a result of these failed efforts to restore decaying empires.

While the numbers are lower than imperialism, communism, and nationalism, racist belief systems, broadly defined to encompass racism, ethnocentrism, and tribalism, have also been a major cause of mass killing since the dawn of human history. These ideas have been spawned by the reality that the world is divided into an almost limitless number of groups. People classify themselves and others according to race, ethnicity, skin color, tribal affiliation, nationality, religion, political beliefs, and endless other distinctions. While most of these categorizations are more artificial than real, people generally attach a great deal of importance to them. They use such classifications to enhance their own group's identity and to debase people from competing groups. These negative views about others can and do easily escalate to extremes, in which a people see others as a threat to their way of life and inevitably begin killing them.

Racism, narrowly defined, "is the belief that different races possess distinct characteristics, abilities, or qualities, especially so as to distinguish them as inferior or superior to one another."[7] The most murderous expression of racism can be found in the global slave trade. The slave trade was premised upon a very racist set of attitudes held by whites, i.e., that Black Africans were subhuman and not deserving of the respect of the whites or Arabs that enslaved them and worked them to death. This perspective allowed slave traders to pursue the most violent and exploitive actions imaginable. Black Africans were captured in Africa and transported on foot, via caravan, or on ships to the location where they would be forced into slavery. The Mideast and the North Atlantic slave trades led to the deaths of over thirty million people.[8]

Ethnic and tribal killing, especially in Africa has also taken the lives of millions. Tribal hatreds reflect the worst kind of in-group/out-group thinking. They consistently spawn orgies of violence which have resulted in huge death tolls.[9]

The next most important ideological driver of mass violence throughout history has been religious conflict, especially that fostered by Islam and Christianity. Religiously motivated mass murder by and among these two religions has killed tens of millions of people over the last two millennia. For the most part, it has been driven by two behaviors that lead religions and religious leaders to instigate and support mass killing.[10]

The first behavior is the drive to maintain ideological purity and discipline in the face of heresies, apostasies, and schisms. Because religious authority rests on claims of textual inerrancy and divine revelations that can never be verified, the veracity and the sustainability of religious beliefs are tenuous at best. Competing ideas can and do arise easily; and when they do, they can threaten the viability of core religious beliefs.

Further, since all religions have experienced internal disagreements about core beliefs, it is not unusual for substantial numbers of followers to break off from the original religion to form new sects. This reality has made religious leaders aggressive in demanding that believers adhere strictly, and without reservation, to established ideological principles. Those who have heretical or schismatic tendencies are inevitably punished, using sometimes-draconian and brutal methods.

The second behavior is the desire to eliminate alternative beliefs. Most religions proclaim that theirs is the one true faith and that their beliefs are the ultimate truths. Since other religions usually make the same claims, the competition to demonstrate the superiority of one religious ideology over another is intense. Throughout history, conservative religionists have often taken strong actions to make their belief systems dominant over all others, including the forcible conversion of non-believers, genocidal killing of people who belong to other religions, and the wholesale destruction of their churches, temples, and idols.In either case, the desire to keep believers toeing the ideological line has a strong tendency to promote violence both within and across religions. Most religious mass killing flows from the intense competition to control believers and keep them within the fold.

So far, I have focused only on large scale mass killing and its relationship to ideology. However, as distressing as that has been, the bad news does not stop with the number killed. The brutality and barbarity that accompany most mass killing incidents are far beyond anything most people can conceptualize. The extreme cruelty with which people have been tortured and killed during the outpourings of mass murder is just plain incomprehensible. One would think that, for a perpetrator, taking someone's life would be seen as sufficient punishment for whatever trumped up crimes were committed by the victims.

But this is not the case. In almost every instance of mass killing, survivors and eyewitnesses have reported that there have been extreme examples of harsh and vicious torture and brutality. Victims were routinely beaten, mutilated, and maimed. They were stoned, flogged, burned, and hacked to death. They were starved, worked until they collapsed and died. They were crucified. They were repeatedly raped or forced into prostitution. There was simply no limit to the pain that could be inflicted on the victims and no restraints on the brutality of the deaths that mass murderers could invent. And what has been described here is but a small sample of these atrocities.

If there is ever to be an end to this grotesque brutality, people must move beyond thinking of these cases of extreme violence as some abstract accounting of human cruelty and actually imagine themselves experiencing death in this manner. People need to feel empathy for the excruciating pain and terror that the victims have experienced and recognize that these atrocities happened to ordinary people, and, sadly, were usually performed by ordinary people run amok. This kind of brutality is not just from some ancient and primitive past or conducted by savages or sub-humans. It has occurred repeatedly in supposedly civilized societies throughout history up to the present day.

Further, the suffering caused during these incidents does not stop when the murder and brutality ends. The aftereffects and side effects of mass killing are much greater than most people imagine. The death totals and the kinds of deaths experienced during large scale mass murders are clearly horrifying; and the suffering experienced by those who lost loved ones is truly awful; but there is, unfortunately, much more. Survivors experience serious follow-on consequences and continuing psychological agony well after the mass killing has died down.

The killings have often led to significant famines because farmers were either being murdered, forcibly conscripted to fight, or obliged to flee their lands to avoid the violence and plundering armies. Normal food production and distribution often ceased and mass starvation was the result. In fact, in many of these cases, such as in Ethiopia during the Dergue control of the country, more than twice as many people died from famine and disease as from the violent conflict and armed struggle.[11]

The murders and violence have frequently forced people to abandon their homes in large numbers and migrate to other countries, as happened after Sunni-Shiite conflicts in Iraq and Syria. Those who fled had no alternative but to settle in refugee camps, where they lived in squalid circumstances, where disease was rampant, and where armed bands often roamed the camps, robbing, brutalizing, and raping the inhabitants. Again, as with the case of extended famine, the numbers of people who were dispossessed has often significantly exceeded the number killed. It is not unusual for millions of people to flee for safety during these orgies of violence. For example, according to the United Nations Refugee Agency, during the period from 2005-2014, an average of forty-five million people were displaced by war each year.[12]

There is also the ongoing fear and terror among the survivors. They worried that they could be the next to die a brutal death, given the usual randomness of the killing that occurred during and after the outbreaks of mass violence. There were, as well, increased levels of aggression and hostility in formerly peaceful societies. The experience of high levels of violence often became the new norm for society, as happened when the Muslim leaders of West Pakistan sent their army into Bangladesh and slaughtered an enormous number of Hindus and Bengali Muslims. Even after the Indian army drove the West Pakistanis out of their country, the killings created palpable fear and distrust within Bangladesh that lasted long after the violence had ended. People, especially women and children, experienced high levels of post-traumatic stress and continued to suffer ongoing psychological consequences.[13]

There were also powerful feelings of humiliation and a strong desire for retribution among those who survived. This led to frequent revenge killings to right the wrongs done, sometimes long after the original violence occurred. Even decades and centuries later, old hatreds festered and did not go away. Inevitably, a demagogue seeking power and influence over the population would remind people of the suffering and humiliation that their ancestors experienced at the hands of a mass killer and then use those memories to instigate another round of violence. For example, during World War II, the Croats ethnically cleansed millions of Serbians. That action became a justification for Serbian violence against

　　　　　　　　　　　　　　　PATH TO POWER, ROAD TO RUIN

Croats four decades later. It was a clear case of violence begetting more violence.

While the mass killing and its follow-on impacts are arguably the most serious consequence of embracing ideologies, they are not the only ones that we have to consider. There are five additional ways that belief systems have caused significant human suffering and led to dire consequences.

First, ideologies' single most deadly consequence, after mass killing, is their role in fostering seemingly unending conflicts between already contentious groups. This kind of conflict occurs between two directly competing and irreconcilable belief systems, as they struggle to remain or become the dominant force in a society or a sphere of influence. Given the substantial perceived differences in beliefs, it is extremely difficult for either side to find common ground; and the hatred that results is so great that any concession to the other side is seen as a catastrophic loss. These types of ideologically-driven conflicts are enduring, brutal and difficult to eradicate. They have resulted in repeated wars, loss of life, waste of resources, and needless human suffering.

Some of these ongoing struggles have evolved over the years to a point where they have as much to do with basic rights, job opportunities, equality of treatment, proper representation in legislative bodies, and rights to territory as they do with ideological preoccupations. But, regardless, the people fighting these battles still line up along ideologically-driven divides. The presence of substantial belief system differences merely inflames tensions and makes it harder to reconcile or negotiate, because people fear being dominated by the other group's ideology and view any defeat as cataclysmic. The two most deadly examples of this phenomenon are the seventy-year conflicts between Jews and Muslims in the Middle East and between Muslims and Hindus in India and Pakistan.

Jews (Israelis) and Muslims (Arabs and Palestinians) have fought four full-blown wars and several smaller clashes. The conflicts have been about Israel's right to exist as an independent state, Israel's control of territory in the West Bank, Gaza, and the Golan Heights, and Israel's ability to prevent Palestinians, who were expelled from Israel, from returning and living there.

The first Arab-Israeli War began in 1948, as five Arab countries invaded the former Palestinian Mandate shortly after Israel's declaration of statehood. The Israelis prevailed and displaced as many as seven hundred thousand Palestinians from their homeland. The second war began in 1967, when Israel, under the threat of Arab invasion, launched a preemptive war against Egypt, Syria, and Jordan and seized substantial Arab territory. The third war started in 1973, with by a surprise invasion of Israel by several Arab countries, which eventually resulted in an Israeli victory.

The most recent war commenced in October 2023 when a large group of Hamas fighters entered Israel and embarked on a killing spree that left over one thousand Israelis dead and many taken as hostages. Israel responded with lethal force, invading Gaza with the intent of killing Hamas leaders, destroying its bases, and eliminating it as a fighting force, killing tens of thousands in the process. Iran and Hezbollah have also entered the fray, shooting hundreds of missiles into Israel and arming their proxies to shell Israel from the border areas.

Unfortunately, the wars do not tell the whole story. During the last seventy years, the Palestinians (operating in the Palestinian Territories), Hamas (operating out of Gaza), and Hezbollah (operating out of Lebanon) have used terrorist tactics, like suicide bombings and rocket attacks, to attempt to compel Israel to accept a negotiated settlement of all issues. Israel has always responded with frequent and decisive military incursions into Palestinian territories to halt the fighting and degrade Arab fighting power. Israel has consistently prevailed in these conflicts but it has been unwilling to make any concessions, especially those which it believes will undermine its strategic position. No peace settlement to end the conflict has ever been reached, as neither side has been willing to budge on any of the key issues that bedevil the relationship.

Hindus (India) and Muslims (Pakistan) have also waged multiple wars since the two countries were partitioned in 1947. At that time, India was split into two separate countries because many Muslims did not want to live under majority Hindu rule. Areas that were predominantly Muslim became East and West Pakistan and the Hindu-majority areas remained as India. Since that time, India and Pakistan have waged war three times over the disputed territory of Kashmir, in 1947, 1965, and 1991, and once more when India invaded East Pakistan to stop the West Pakistani genocide of Bengali Muslims and Hindus in 1971. The hatred between the two sides is palpable; and the threat of war continues as there have been many armed actions, without any permanent resolution of the hostilities.

Second, ideologies' ability to inflame and prolong ideological conflict does not represent the limits of the harm that these belief systems can inflict. Disruptive ideologies have consistently and systematically blocked mankind's progress towards developing a more just society and a more harmonious world order. There have been three times in the last century when mankind has had an opportunity to coalesce around some type of global worldview for the benefit of all humanity but has failed to do so because of ideological intrusion.

After World War I, which led to an estimated fifteen million civilian and military deaths, people were more open than ever before to finding a way to end to war and conflict.[14] One result was the formation of the League of Nations, which attempted to unite humans around a program for peace. But this effort to create a better world order was destroyed by the rise of three illiberal ideologies, i.e., ultra-nationalism, fascism, and communism. These ideas turned out to be very successful and spread very quickly to Russia, Germany, Japan, and Italy in the 1920's and 1930's, eventually becoming the leading political force in those countries. All these nations became aggressively imperialistic, seeking to dominate and control other nations, and ultimately leading them into yet another world war.

The Second World War proved to be even more bloody than the First World War, as an estimated sixty-six million people, at least half of whom were civilians, are thought to have been killed.[15] This tidal wave of death and human suffering and the complete defeat of Japan and Germany, the principal instigators of the conflict, created another opportunity to develop a global organization for peace, i.e., the United Nations. The hope was that such a movement could help put an end to conflict, induce nations and peoples to coalesce around a common worldview, and embrace, for once and for all, mankind's common humanity.

But, here again, communism continued to spread during the last half of the twentieth century, moving beyond Russia to Korea, China, Southeast Asia and Eastern Europe. This led to a Cold War conflict between communism and capitalism that lasted for another four decades. When that was resolved, it appeared as though mankind was going to unite around the liberal world order, with extensive global trade, free cross-border movement, multi-lateral cooperation, acceptance of mankind's common humanity, and respect for freedom and individualism. The hope was that these ideals might prevail over absolutism, tyranny, and parochialism.

Unfortunately, those prospects have not materialized, with more and more countries slipping away from democracy to dictatorship. Militant religions, nationalism, and racism have come to the fore in many nations, further dividing mankind once again. The power of these illiberal ideologies to capture people's minds, play upon their fears and anxieties, reinforce instinctive prejudices, and disrupt rational thought processes has continued to block mankind's ability to progress to new more advanced forms of society.

Third, besides prolonging and intensifying conflict and blocking humanity's forward progress, the next most deadly consequence of embracing ideologies occurs when an ideology has no competition, completely controls a society, and then moves toward totalitarian governance. In this situation, it brooks no dissent or deviation from established orthodoxy and completely dominates society for an extended period of time. Inevitably, the ideological rigidity leads to the complete stultification of and, sometimes, brings about the internal collapse or complete degradation of the countries involved. This precludes any social, cultural, economic or technological advancement for decades, even centuries. The Roman Catholic Church in the Middle Ages and the Soviet Union in the years from 1917 to 1989 provide relevant examples.

The Roman Catholic Church exercised total ideological control and domination of Western European society for one thousand years. Kings and Princes obeyed its dictates. Ordinary people lived in utter fear of the Church and slavishly followed its rules. The Church tolerated no dissent and no alternative ways of thinking, using sometimes grotesque violence to ensure obedience to its dictates. It drove all competing ideologies out of existence and suppressed all philosophical, literary, artistic, and scientific expression and advancement. The result: European society made relatively little social, technological, or economic progress from the Fourth Century, when the Church first became the state religion of the Roman Empire, until its absolute power was moderated during the Reformation in the Sixteenth Century. Mankind's intellectual development, artistic progress, and scientific advancement were frozen in place for a millennium.

The USSR also endured an extended period of brutal totalitarian rule, in which the government controlled everything people did, said, and even thought. Communist leaders killed, tortured, and imprisoned millions to achieve their utopian vision for society. Anyone who did not toe the ideological line or who represented a potential threat to the regime was eliminated. In doing so, the leaders crushed the life out of the society, put an end to innovation and creativity, and drained the motivation and energy of the citizenry. As a result, the nation and its vassal states in Central and Eastern Europe and West Asia became non-competitive with capitalist democracies and had to undergo massive restructuring when Soviet rule ended.

The fourth way in which ideologies disrupt society is by polarizing competing groups within a society. Even when there is no mass murder, no civil war or violent conflict, and no totalitarian repression, divisions along ideological lines can wreck a nation. It happens when irreconcilable belief systems within a country create the full-blown polarization of that society. In the United States, for example, competing and incompatible ideologies, e.g., conservative Christianity vs secular humanism, white supremacism vs. racial, ethnic, and gender equality, and social conservatism vs. social liberalism, struggle to dominate the nation in which they both operate. Since the opposing views are equally represented in the country, the entire society has become deadlocked, making it unable to function or advance. Each side strives for total control of society. Neither side will relinquish or modify its ideological stance, work toward joint solutions, or adopt a "live and let live" approach to each other's beliefs. The result in the United States is that the U.S. government has been completely paralyzed and the nation remains hopelessly divided, much to its own detriment.

Finally, ideologies can become the basis for justifying the complete suppression of one societal group by another, so much so, that it never becomes a force to be contended with in society. The outcome is accomplished by using terror to exercise complete control of the targeted group, and then systematically depriving that group of all the rights, privileges, and opportunities normally accorded a citizen of a given country.

White Supremacists' harsh racist domination of African-Americans in the southern United States lasted for the one hundred years following the end of the American Civil War and slavery. The unfounded fear and hatred of Black Americans was sustained by a supremacist ideology that claimed that Blacks were inferior to whites, were dirty and unclean, represented competition for jobs and economic opportunities, and threatened white privilege and safety.

As a result, white supremacists deprived the former slaves and their descendants of access to the full range of rights and opportunities accorded citizens of the United States and subjected them to the harshest repression imaginable. Black Americans were completely isolated from white southern society and not allowed to share public facilities on an equal basis. They were denied the most basic rights; never given equal standing before the law; not allowed to vote (even though the Constitution granted them that right); prevented from attending white schools and universities; and punished for daring to speak out or for failing to show proper deference to whites.

They were systematically excluded from any opportunity to advance themselves beyond their very subservient status. They could not ever raise themselves to the level of white men in society. If they did, they were beaten back down. Further, all of these restrictions and exclusions were enforced violently through extra-judicial killing, lynching, castration, beatings, and false imprisonment. Black Americans were terrorized into submission.

Yet another egregious example of depriving people the right to a full life is the caste system that strangled India for millennia. The caste system, which is generally accepted to be more than three thousand years old, divided Hindus into rigid hierarchical groups, based on work and duty. It segregated the people of India into five main categories and assigned each to a specific set of occupations: Brahmins— priests and teachers; Kshatriyas—warriors and rulers; Vaishyas—farmers, traders, and merchants; Shudras—laborers; and Outcastes—street sweepers and latrine cleaners.

> "The Indian caste system is said to be stable and unquestioned by those within it, bound as it is by religion and the Hindu belief in reincarnation, the belief that one lives out this life in the karma of the previous ones, suffers the punishment or reaps the reward for one's deeds in a past life and that the more keenly one follows the rules for the caste they were born to, the higher the station will be in the next life... Some observers says this distinguishes the Indian caste system from any other, that people in the lowest caste system accept their lot, that it is fixed and unbending, that the Dalits must live out their karma decreed by the Gods..."[16]

This thinking has guaranteed the permanent repression of whole segments of the population, a reality from which they could never escape.

It should be clear from this consequences review that ideologies can be very disruptive of the smooth functioning of society, fostering hatreds and sustained conflict, blocking constructive change, reinforcing mankind's worst instincts, and marginalizing people who are consciously excluded from the mainstream of society. They consistently produce terrible outcomes.

Chapter 3

IDEOLOGY DRIVERS

When analyzing the consequences that flow from the implementation of history's most consequential belief systems, it becomes evident that it does not matter whether one is talking about Communist or Fascist states, Christian or Islamic theocracies, nationalist or imperialistic powers, or the multitude of different antagonistic racial, ethnic, or tribal groups that have populated the world throughout history. The same mass killing, violent conflict, and systemic repression occurs repeatedly across all these ideologies, regardless of the specific content of their belief systems. The unpleasant outcomes have not been the special province of a particular ideology, creed, or doctrine. Rather, they are common to all.

The fact that such radically different belief systems have produced such similar end results is surprising because the major ideologies discussed here usually claim that their beliefs are both unique and inerrant. The only way we could keep getting the same consequences would be if the ideologies share common underlying drivers that cut across all the ideologies, overpowering the obvious differences in their creeds and doctrines. And, in fact, when we dig deeper, there do appear to be three common drivers that are effectively the building blocks of all these belief systems. We can discover these drivers by studying the motivations that compel people to accept these ideologies in the first place.

Ideologies are really designed to attract a following, gain their commitment to a set of ideas, and establish a power structure that allows the leaders to pursue whatever agenda they want. Ideologies are tools of justification, used to validate leaders' agendas and programs. To be able to persuade people to support them, leaders must be able to gain the attention, commitment, and loyalty of their followers. The key is to have a highly motivated group that will do the leader's bidding. This is where the ideologies come into play.

The ideology is the motivational tool that captures prospective followers' interests and imagination and causes them to subscribe to the belief system. The doctrine and dogma then are primarily there to provide the structure, the rules, and the standards that lock followers into the belief structure.

The success of ideologies has resulted from their ability of attract followers with need- based rather than dogmatic appeals. Ideologies, using need and fear-driven strategies, have been remarkably effective at gathering large numbers of adherents and retaining them for very long periods of time. In some cases, they have attracted millions, hundreds of millions, and even billions of followers worldwide. We know that more than two and a quarter billion people currently identify themselves as Christian and hold Christian beliefs[1] while over two billion people are presently loyal followers of Islam, adhering to the rules laid out in the religion's sacred texts, the Koran and the Hadith.[2] We also know that a quarter of the world's population, about one to one and a half billion people, lived under a communist regime in the latter half of the twentieth century[3]; and we estimate, that at any given time, a substantial percentage, maybe a majority, of humanity has readily embraced nationalistic, imperialistic, racist, and ethnocentric belief systems.

The fact that need-based ideologies can gain and retain followers on such a large scale demonstrates the power of human needs as a motivator of people. There has been significant research on and analysis of this subject, dating back several decades. In a 1943 paper entitled, *A Theory of Human Motivation*, Abraham Maslow postulated that there was indeed a hierarchy of human needs that drove human behavior. His theory has remained a leading hypothesis in the field of psychology up to the present day. Maslow's famous needs-based framework identified five principal categories of human need that applied to all peoples, including:

• "Basic physiological needs, including food, water, sleep, sex, comfort, and stability of bodily processes."

• "Existential needs for safety, including security of body, employment, resources, morality, family, health, and property."

• "Relational needs, including love, belonging, friendship, family, and sexual intimacy"

• "Esteem needs, including self-esteem, confidence, achievement, respect of others and by others."

• "Self-actualization, which goes beyond the first four categories to embrace a higher order of thinking and living, where psychological and emotional needs become secondary."[4]

While Maslow created a core human motivational framework, many other scholars have expanded on it and developed new applications over the last several decades. For example, social psychologists, like John Jost and colleagues, have identified a modified needs-based framework to explain the relationship between the acceptance of religious and political ideologies and human needs. He, and others, demonstrated, through research, that the adoption of ideologies does indeed drive from three specific human motives. He tells us that: "Ideologies arise from epistemic, existential, and relational motives to reduce uncertainty, threat, and social discord."[5]

Existential Motives: People strongly desire to mitigate their substantial existential and death anxiety. Humans seek relief from this misery by embracing belief systems that provide an escape from their fears and anxieties, protection from the vicissitudes of this world, and the promise of a utopian outcome to this life, either in the here and now, or in paradise in the next world.

Epistemic Motives: People dread the thought of facing an uncertain world without a well-defined set of rules. So, they reach for a fixed and unalterable set of principles that can anchor their daily existence and free them from the responsibility of making life decisions. The need for certainty and structure makes them more willing to submit to absolutist religious or political ideologies which promise to eliminate doubt and uncertainty from their lives.

Relational Motives: Many people in this world lack adequate self-esteem and a strong sense of self-worth. They can most easily remedy this problem by finding a life purpose and/or group affiliation that will make them feel special and part of something much greater than themselves. Joining groups with whom they share common values and beliefs, that have already established themselves as superior, can boost their self-esteem and give them the security of belonging to something great. Then, self-esteem can be "obtained, and subsequently maintained, by living up to the standards of value that are part of the social roles inhabited by individuals in the context of their cultures…"[6]

These three categories of need are central to understanding the popularity of the leading belief systems. Each is deeply woven into the fundamental teachings and principles of the most widely accepted political and religious ideologies. They have specifically been tailored to attract followers by eliminating their fears, increasing their well-being, providing certainties they can count on, and boosting their self-worth. Each ideology addresses these core needs in a different way.

Certain religious belief systems, like Islam and Christianity, assuage the fear of death and reduce existential anxiety by promising eternal life in paradise for those who faithfully obey their rules. They build their loyal supporters' self-esteem by telling them that God loves them. They reduce doubt and uncertainty by offering their followers the security and certainty of a supposedly inerrant doctrine, that is promulgated by an omniscient and omnipotent God. They create communities of like-minded believers to give their followers a sense of belonging by establishing places of worship where all can pray together.

National Socialism mixed rabid nationalism and racism, and, in the process, promised a different kind of earthly utopia. Adolph Hitler gave Germans hope by promising that he would create a new German empire and restore Germany's national pride. He assured his people that he would conquer and eliminate Germany's enemies, i.e., the Jews, the Slavs, and the Bolsheviks. He said he would create a racial utopia that would hold only people of Aryan blood, with all inferior races and people being destroyed, enslaved, or relocated. Hitler inflated the identity of the German people by telling Germans that they were the "Master Race" and were destined to rule the world. Hitler promised that the uncertainty and chaos that had characterized the years before he came to power would be a thing of the past and that order and justice would prevail. He would make this happen by ruling with absolute and unchallenged power.

Imperialist leaders used their conquests of less developed countries to increase their citizens' wealth and prosperity, by creating new markets for their goods and services and providing access to cheap labor and raw materials. They established and restored a real sense of pride among their people by showing them that they were part of a great empire, one that was destined to last for a long time. And they gave their followers a

　　　　PATH TO POWER, ROAD TO RUIN

sense of security and the certainty that stemmed from the nation's ability to overpower and dominate the inferior others they had conquered, thus positioning themselves at the top of the global racial and national hierarchy.

Studying these ideologies from the perspective of how well they have apparently served human wishes/desires and relieved human fears/anxieties, it is easy to see how people could develop a very positive view of these belief systems. They appear, in all respects, to be giving ordinary people the things they desperately want and need, while, at the same time, providing leaders with the motivational tools they require to get people to accept their ideas and endorse their agendas. Such an apparently beneficial outcome for both parties has likely encouraged people to more readily embrace their use.

We already know that belief systems have been astoundingly effective at accumulating large numbers of followers. As indicated above, they have been successful primarily for two reasons. First, they have tailored their appeals to address people's most critical needs, desires, fears and anxieties. Second, the ideologies' belief structures have specifically been designed not only to gain a following, but also to provide solutions that address the specific problems that people have in their lives and want solved. When you look at it this way, you see that there are really three different kinds of ideology drivers, each supported by a common set of needs and their associated ideas.

The first group of ideology drivers are those that are expressly designed to address humanity's most significant existential anxieties. Utopian belief systems, like communism, Christianity, and Islam, neutralize these worries by promising to create an ideal outcome to this life, either by restructuring society in ways that would make this life easier to endure or by convincing people they will go to paradise in the next life if they are faithful and obedient followers.

The second group of ideology drivers are those that are designed to give people the certainties they need to cope with life by providing absolute, unchallengeable truths on which they can anchor their lives. Strict, uncompromising versions of absolutist ideologies, like fundamentalist religions, eliminate all doubts and uncertainty by postulating and enforcing a set of non-negotiable, inflexible, and indisputable principles that all followers must accept in their entirety or experience serious consequences.

The third group of drivers are those that are explicitly structured to give people a strong sense of self-worth and belonging. Supremacist ideologies, like nationalism and imperialism, tell followers that they are part of a great nation and that they are superior to all others because of their affiliation with that country. Similarly, supremacist belief systems, like racism and ethnocentrism, elevate one particular class of humans by raising their group's status and simultaneously lowering that of all others. These supremacist ideologies provide people with significant reasons to feel better about themselves.

What this analysis shows is that there are three distinct need categories--relieving existential anxiety, removing uncertainty and doubt, and building identity and belonging--and that there are three specific types of solutions to these anxieties--utopian outcomes, absolutist belief positions, and supremacist stances with regard to others. These solutions--utopianism, absolutism, and supremacism--are the core ideas that represent the essence of ideologies studied here.

If we look at ideologies in this way, we can get different insights than if we just study the ideology from the perspective of the ideas that go to make up a belief system. If we skip the doctrine and dogma that we were all brought up with, we can see more clearly what ultimately drives the ideology. This enables us to understand why it leads to the consequences that materialize when it takes over people's minds. When we categorize ideologies by motives, including needs, desires, fears, anxieties, stemming from humans' responses to their environment, we find that the ideologies are more similar than dissimilar. They are just different narratives to tell what is essentially the same story.

It is important to recognize that the three most basic, motive-driven ideology drivers subsume all the rest and have been part of human culture for millennia. They are not new or even original ideas, existing long before the ideologies, that later co-opted them, came into being. They became the foundation of belief systems, like communism, conservative religions, imperialism, nationalism, and racism because of the leverage they had with potential followers and their ability to address people's life problems.

They represent the umbrella that covers all ideologies. Don't think about communism, nationalism, imperialism, and racism or Christianity, Islam, Judaism, Hinduism, and Buddhism. Think instead about the three fundamental drivers—the utopian, absolutist, and supremacist ideas that underpin and subsume all of them.

Then by analyzing each of these three drivers separately, as I

                    PATH TO POWER, ROAD TO RUIN

do in the next three chapters of this book, we can gain insight into the vulnerability and consequences of the ideologies they support. Such understanding is otherwise hard to obtain because the belief systems' doctrines, creeds, and dogmas only obscure ideologies' true meaning and mislead people who are being asked to buy into a set of premises without really comprehending them. These three in-depth analyses will make the case that the three ideas and the ideologies they support are of limited validity. They need to be discarded as belief systems in favor of other alternatives, several of which are proposed in the final chapter of this book.

Chapter 4

UTOPIANISM: HEAVEN CAN WAIT

Utopia is an imagined state where everything is perfect. In utopia, all the suffering, conflicts, injustices, and troubles of this world will be gone and people will be able to live in peace and harmony forever.

The concept of an ideally perfect life or society, where people find ultimate happiness, is one that generates enormous human interest. Whether the conversation is about utopias of this world, the next world, or just figments of the human imagination, it is clear that dreaming about and bringing about the perfect society or perfect world has been an important preoccupation of mankind for several thousand years. Utopian ideas are present in all human cultures in all parts of the world and have taken on a multitude of different forms. They have been expressed as literary masterpieces, philosophical treatises, religious or political ideologies and movements, or even personal dreams or wishes.

Tellingly, they are not dying out. Utopian visions of all types continue to form and grow and preoccupy all humanity, almost to the point of obsession. The omnipresence of these concepts is a testimony to the power these ideas have over people and how utterly essential they seem to be. There is indeed an intense human need to believe that, somewhere and someday, we will live in a better, safer, more forgiving world than the one we live in today.

The impetus for the obsession with these ideas has been the difficulty of life itself. For the majority of people who have lived on this earth, life has been an experience filled with seemingly unending trials.

Our world has been ravaged by the awesome destructive power of nature with its earthquakes, devastating storms, and floods, as well as its deadly infestations and plagues. As a people, we have been victimized by constant war and violence, brutal tyranny, and mass murder. We experience backbreaking work and seemingly endless toil just to provide the most basic necessities of life. We are and have been at the whim of unpredictable and uncontrollable economic and societal forces that can, in an instant, devastate our financial and emotional security; we have felt the pain of isolation and loneliness; and we have been subject to the rampant inequities and injustices of a world that is not concerned with the fair and equal distribution of life circumstances and benefits. And, finally, after we go through our lives, we face the relentless, terrifying certainty of our own death as well as the deaths of our loved ones and friends.

So, it is not surprising that we dream of a release from this agony and fantasize about the possibility of a better world, where there is no suffering, no conflict, no injustice, no want, and no fear. We desperately need to believe that this life can be better, that doubt and uncertainty can be removed, that the burdens we carry can be lifted from our shoulders, and that we and our loved ones will be safe from danger. We want to know that there will be some relief from the harshness of this life, some reward for a life well lived, and some justice or recompense for the grossly unequal way in which suffering is distributed throughout and across societies.

Demagogues, social reformers, political activists, religious proselytizers, and aspiring leaders have long recognized humans' extreme vulnerability to these wishes and dreams. By promising to deliver a better world, they have been able to persuade people to join forces with them and help them pursue their religious, political, and social agendas. The utopian narratives that they have used to advance their causes and gain influence have undergone a slow but significant evolution over the last three thousand years.

The earliest streams of utopian thought envisioned ideal worlds that existed in another time and place. Some of these utopias, like the Bible's Garden of Eden or the Golden Age, as described in Hesiod's *Work and Days*, were believed to have existed in the distant past at the beginning of time, when the first race of men was created, before mankind sinned. Others were thought to be present in the here and now in some remote corner of the world, like Shangri-la, Atlantis, or Cockaigne.

Regardless of when they were conceived or how they were described, all of these utopias were just mythical conceptions constructed by humans, merely the wishes of a long-suffering species. They were part of a powerful human drive to imagine alternative worlds that were specifically designed to help mitigate, however little, the agonies of this life—the suffering, the hardship, and the loss.

For the most part, the earliest of these utopias were lands of sensual gratification. They were problem-free worlds where there would be no toil, effort, or conflict. They would be places where food and drink were in abundance, where every desire was satisfied, where pain and suffering were eradicated, where toil and strife were a thing of the past, where all people lived in harmony, and where death was banished forever.

"The Islands of the Blest," written by the Roman poet, Horace, in the first century BCE, provides one example of the genre:

> "Let us seek the fields, the happy fields and island of the blest, where the earth is not plowed, but yearly yields the grain, and the vine is not trimmed, but forever flourishes, and the branch of the olive never fails to blossom, and the black fig, ungrafted, adorns its own tree, honey drips from the hollow oak, from the lofty hills, the light-stepping spring comes splashing down. There the goats need no orders to come to the milking pails, and the flock returns gladly with swelling udders, and the bear does not growl as he circles the sheep field at evening, and the earth does not swell up with vipers."[1]

Another example from medieval times, written by Telecleides, describes the land of Cockaigne, a land of luxury where everything anyone needs is close at hand and where there is no suffering:

> "In Cockaigne, we eat and drink freely without care and sweat; the food is choice and the wine is clear at fourses and supper time…under heaven no land like this of such joy and endless bliss." "There [is] many a sweet sight. Everything is day; and there is no night. There [is] no quarreling nor strife. There [is] no death, but endless life. There [is] no lack of food or cloth. There [is] no man or woman wroth."[2]

These literary visions of paradise were merely wishes for a better world, offered without any proposal for how this new world would be achieved and without any action plan to achieve the intended outcome in this world. But that reality was soon to change.

The second stream of utopian thought exploited these early literary ideas and concentrated on the prospect of finding a real paradise, not in the here and now, but in the next life, after death. Utopias of the

next world have always been inextricably tied up with religion and were
based on three unverifiable and unfalsifiable beliefs: that there is an
invisible spirit world operating behind the visible world where humans
live, that every man has a soul or spirit that lives on after the body dies,
and that there is a world, separate from this one, where souls reside after
death.

We know that mankind has believed that life continued after
death for more than three thousand years. However, it was only in
the centuries leading up to the early Christian Era that certain groups
began to believe that life after death could in fact be pleasurable and
was something to be sought after. Prior to that time, most Egyptians,
Mesopotamians, Greeks, Romans, and Jews thought that the afterlife was
a shadow world where the shades or souls of men resided. Kings, heroes,
and the elite might be able to achieve immortality and a life with the
Gods in the hereafter. But, for most people, the world of the dead was a
bleak, unhappy place.

The early Egyptians supposed that, after the body died, the "ka"
or soul wandered in the real world and continued to do much as it had
done in life, scrounging for food and drink and experiencing sorrows,
fears and regret. It was not a pleasant existence. Only the Pharaohs and
the Royal Family had a chance at a different fate. They could, if they
proved worthy, join the Gods in the starry heaven. For most of Egyptian
history, the masses of people were taught that they had no such choice.
However, by the latter stages of the Egyptian empire, increasing numbers
of people believed that a more pleasant form of life after death was
possible for all who lived a just existence, regardless of their station in life.

In Mesopotamia, the world of the dead was even more depressing
and dark. The soul passed through a judgment process after death in
which its fate was determined by the generosity of its offerings and
sacrifices made during its life. But all souls suffered in the afterlife,
regardless of the type of life they lived. The virtuous just suffered less.

The early Greeks and Romans believed that the dead passed
into the underworld, where they were just shadows that lacked feeling
or awareness and wandered aimlessly. There was no happy afterlife, no
reward or punishment for a life well or poorly lived. However, with the
rise of the Orphic cults in the centuries just before the beginning of the
Christian era, the Greek view changed. For the cultists, the afterlife could
be pleasant.

For the Jews, belief in a utopian paradise for the dead is not central to the religion. The Old Testament contains almost no mention of life after death except in a couple of books written closer to the Christian era. Today, there are many different streams of thought about the afterlife in Judaism, with some feeling there will be a resurrection of the dead when the messiah returns and others rejecting the idea altogether.

As the examples above illustrate, the concept of a wonderful afterlife or heavenly paradise didn't represent an important part of the belief structure of most ancient civilizations or their religions. It was really Christianity that popularized the idea of a paradise in the next world, a place where the righteous would go to live in peace with God after their death. Christians thought that paradise was a real place, as did the adherents of Islam several hundred years later.

The concept of a pleasant afterlife gained credibility because people began to believe that there must be rewards for a life well lived, for the sacrifices required to be a righteous person, for the effort to purify oneself through discipline, denial, restraint and hard work, for special service given to advance religion's position in the world, or for the willingness to lay down one's life for one's God. They believed that there must be some explanation for the huge differences in suffering, pain, and the difficulty of people's lives. There had to be some compensation for the bad things that happened to so many people.

Heaven was offered as the solution to these existential problems. The heavenly paradise was postulated to exist because it fulfilled the desire of all people to believe that there is an ideal and pleasant outcome to this life and because it gave prospective religious leaders an important tool to attract large numbers of new followers.

But what was heaven going to be like? Unfortunately, that question is answered only in the most basic terms by most religions. Much is left up to the human imagination because relatively little is written about exactly what heaven might be like. And this may have been a deliberate strategy to allow religious leaders leeway to make it seem as appealing as possible to followers.

In the Old Testament, heaven, it turns out, is much like the ancients' conceptions of paradise—a land of "milk and honey." Two examples are instructive:

First from Genesis:

"And the Lord planted a garden eastward in Eden; and there put the man whom he had formed. And out of the ground made the Lord God to grow every tree that is pleasant to the sight and good for food; the Tree of Life also in the midst of the garden; and the Tree of Knowledge of good and evil. And a river went out of Eden to water the Garden…and out of the ground, the Lord God formed every beast of the field and every fowl of the air and brought them to Adam…and he made a woman and brought her unto the man."[3]

Then from the Apocalypse of Baruch:
" And then healing shall descend in dew, and disease shall withdraw, and anxiety and anguish and lamentation shall pass from amongst men, and gladness shall proceed through the whole earth. And no one shall again die untimely, nor shall any adversity suddenly befall. And judgments, and reviling, and contentions, and revenges, and blood, and passions, and envy, and hatred, and whatsoever things are like these shall go into condemnation when they are removed."[4]

The New Testament also has little information about the exact nature of heaven and how it will work. Two passages from the Apocalypse of John constitute most of what is said:
"Therefore are they before the throne of God, and serve him day and night in his temple; and he that sits on the throne shall dwell among them. They shall hunger no more, neither thirst anymore; neither shall the sun light on them, nor any heat. For the Lamb, which is in the midst of the throne shall feed them, and shall lead them unto living fountains of waters; and God shall wipe away from their eyes."[5]

"And I saw a new heaven and a new earth; for the first heaven and the first earth were passed away; and there was no more sea. And I, John, saw the holy city, New Jerusalem, coming down from God out of heaven, prepared as a bride adorned for her husband. And I heard a great voice out of heaven saying, behold the tabernacle of God is with men and he shall dwell with them and they shall be his people, and God himself shall be with them and be their God. And God shall wipe away all tears from their eyes; and there shall be no more death, neither sorrow, nor crying, neither shall there be any more pain, for the former things are passed away."[6]

The Muslim version of heaven is for all intents and purposes just like the Christian concept mentioned above. It is simply a "land of milk and honey" from primitive myths and literature. The passage below is characteristic of the genre.

"But for those that fear the majesty of their Lord there are two gardens…planted with shady trees…each is watered by a flowing spring…each bears every kind of fruit in pairs…they shall recline on couches lined with thick brocade, and within their reach will hang the fruits of both gardens…They shall dwell with bashful virgins whom neither man nor jinnee will have touched before… Virgins as fair as corals and rubies…and beside these there shall be two other gardens of darkest green…A gushing fountain shall flow in each… each planted with fruit trees, the palm and the pomegranate…In each, there shall be virgins chaste and fair… dark eyed virgins sheltered in their tents whom neither man nor jinnee will have touched before…they shall recline on green cushions and rich carpets."[7]

Regardless of which version of the afterlife one embraces, it is important to recognize that, for monotheistic religions, the concept of an otherworldly paradise represented only a slight evolution from the "land of milk and honey" that was generally wished for by the ancients. The actual descriptions of heaven in the Apocrypha and the Koran were very much like those proposed by the ancients in the works of Horace, Telecleides, and the Bible.

There is no evidence to suggest that they reflect some special revelation or insight from divinity or religious leaders. Instead, they merely transferred the location of paradise from some remote time or place in this world to an imagined world said to exist after death, where a monotheistic God would rule beneficently at the end of time.

This altered conception of utopia certainly benefited the high priests, prophets, and other people who made their living pretending to intervene with the God(s) on behalf of humanity. By placing utopia outside of this life, there was no way the concept could be challenged or verified. Further, it released the leaders from any responsibility for delivering on the promised utopia while they were alive. People were taught that they just had to endure this life and wait for the next one to be wonderful.

The only alternative to the versions of heaven proposed by the monotheistic religions are those postulated by Buddhism and Hinduism. For these religions, heaven was meant to be the liberation of man from the endless cycle of suffering, death, and rebirth that is associated with this life. It was the end of existence as humans knew it. It was achieved when, after many dozens, hundreds, or even thousands of rebirths, individuals finally advanced spiritually to the point that they had eliminated attachments, desires, passions, and needs, and no longer needed to pass through this life to transform and purify themselves. They would then have merged with the infinite and achieved Nirvana, which was described as a state of infinite bliss.

Religious leaders were apparently quite happy to postpone the advent of a better life until after death. Fortunately, many philosophers and statesmen were not. They believed they could substantially improve life in this world right now. There was no need to wait. They thought they could, through the use of rational thought processes, design a better society, one that would make this life much better. This type of thinking led to a new wave of utopian thought.

During the third to fifth century BC, a third stream of utopian thinking began to emerge. Greek statesmen, like Solon and Lycurgus, and Greek philosophers, like Socrates and Plato, proposed that men could challenge the conventions by which their societies and their states were run. They believed it was possible to construct new and better ways to govern, which would produce superior outcomes for all. Mankind could, on its own, create a more perfect world, in this life, by transforming society according to a specific set of principles that could be worked out rationally, based on analysis and experience.

In *The Republic*, Plato set about defining the type of state that was required to bring about the perfect society. He created a very detailed and original roadmap for how the state could be restructured to produce a more rational order and a more ideal outcome for day-to-day life. The goal of this effort was not to create a sensual paradise or achieve some sort of heavenly perfection. Instead, the objectives were: to resolve inequities, get rid of corruption, reduce suffering, increase social harmony, create a more just society, and produce a more evolved citizenry. In other words, utopia was more than a dream. It was, according to this line of thinking, something that could be achieved by taking control of one's life and living according to preset guidelines.

Plato was not alone in his effort to maintain that mankind could develop a better world in the here and now. Many authors, especially

                                              PATH TO POWER, ROAD TO RUIN

from the seventeenth century to the present, described models for building a utopian society in this world. Many of those who wrote these treatises were famous in their own right. Saint Thomas More was a respected lawyer, social philosopher, and statesman. Sir Francis Bacon was a famous scientist. B.F. Skinner was an eminent psychologist. Timothy Dwight was a well-known religious leader. Robert Owen and Karl Marx were social and political revolutionaries. Samuel Butler and William Dean Howells were noted authors.

Some of these books were presented in the form of novels, like Huxley's *Brave New World.* Others were written as factual expositions of places that were thought to exist in remote areas of the world, such as Sir Thomas More's *Utopia.* Many, like Timothy Dwight's' *Greenfield Hills,* described small utopian communities that had actually been created in rural areas of the United States and Europe. Other works, like *Mercier's Memory of the Year 2500* or Bellamy's *Looking Backward* were stories from the future about what life might be like one or more centuries hence, when man had advanced to a new stage of wisdom and social development. Some, like Marx and Engels' *Communist Manifesto,* provided considerable analysis of the flaws and contradictions of existing society with prescriptions for major overhaul that would create a new utopian world and a more evolved mankind. And several, such as George Orwell's *Animal Farm* and *1984,* were distinctly non-utopian. They described dystopias that arose from attempts to create a utopia. They were earthly versions of hell that very idea of utopia.[8]

At heart, all these authors were reformers, people seeking to find a way to improve this world on a small or grand scale by suggesting alternative models for how the world might be run. While the utopias proposed were each different in their own way, there were common threads.

Most authors presumed the existence of God as creator and ultimate authority. Most felt that there would be a centralized world government that would manage the economy, deciding what needed to be produced to serve the needs of the populace. Many hypothesized that all industry would be nationalized or at least centralized. Most asserted that each citizen would share all goods equally. In fact, it was presupposed that there would be total equality in all things. Several assumed that the existence of money and trading, of buying and selling, and anything that fed the human tendency toward greed would all disappear. Many also forecasted that things like fashion and style in clothing, jewelry, and other items would be discarded because they tended to incite envy and grasping for more. Many of the systems proposed that social and political ambition and politicians would be eliminated.

Most books of this genre assumed that people would go along with this radical change, that it could be implemented without violence or widespread protest and that a true brotherhood of man would be established naturally in this new world. Others, like Huxley and Skinner, assumed that men would need medication or behavioral programming to adjust to the new society. Only a handful of authors, like Marx and Engels, recognized or admitted that there would be a major and potentially violent transformation of society if mankind were to achieve the desired utopian goals.

Regardless of who wrote them, what genre they belonged to, or what kind of utopia or dystopia they described, they were, for the most part, intellectual exercises. They definitely contributed to efforts to reform some of the ills of society and were part of efforts to eliminate serious abuses like slavery and child labor. Some religiously and morally oriented groups, like the Shakers, the Fourierists, and the Icarians, did go beyond intellectual discourse and started small isolated utopian communities in rural areas during the 18th century. But they were relatively few and far between and none left a lasting legacy.

However, in the 20th century, people began to realize that they could exploit the power and resources of the nation state to effect broad-based societal transformation on a national, regional or even global scale. Given that the concept of utopia addressed such powerful human needs, many revolutionaries saw that, by positioning their ideas and belief systems as capable of fulfilling mankind's wish for utopian outcomes to this life, they could gain tremendous leverage over potential followers. They could use utopian promises to sell their agendas to large numbers of people and seize control of an entire nation, its economic resources, and its military might and then ultimately use that power to effect significant social change.

Marxist/Leninist utopians from various nations, including Russia, China, Cambodia, North Korea, and Vietnam, were the first examples of this new approach. They went beyond the idea of establishing small, utopian experiments. Instead, they initiated large-scale, forcible overhauls of entire nations or regions, with the goal of creating a revolutionary political and social order that would transform both society as a whole and also people, as individuals. They promised to create a paradise on earth, where all the output of society would be shared equally, where class differences and disadvantages would be eradicated, where selfishness and parochial interests would wither away, and where a new and better human would evolve as a result.

Communists sought to create a more egalitarian world by eliminating what they believed to be the principal cause of conflict, oppression, and suffering, i.e., the private ownership of property. In their view, modern society was divided into two distinct groups. The first group were the capitalists who owned the economy's means of production--the factories and machines they acquired to make products; and the second group were the workers they hired to manufacture and distribute those products to customers.

Since the capitalists controlled the wealth generating mechanism of society, they controlled the essential economic resources and how they were allocated. As a result, they could dictate the terms and conditions of employment for the workers. They used their position of power to maximize their wealth by driving down the wages of laborers to the lowest possible point and compelling the workers to accept the most undesirable working conditions, thus impoverishing the working class.

Communism sought to undo this condition and end the exploitation of the working class through a revolt against and the eradication of the bourgeois elites and their private ownership of property.

"We have seen that the first step in the revolution by the working class is to raise the proletariat to the position of ruling class...The proletariat will use its political supremacy to wrest, by degrees, all capital from the bourgeoisie, to centralize all instruments of production in the hands of the state, i.e., the proletariat organized as the ruling class to increase the total of productive forces as rapidly as possible...Of course, in the beginning this cannot be effected except by means of despotic inroads on the rights of property and on the conditions of bourgeois production, by means of measures...which necessitate further inroads upon the old social order, and are unavoidable as a means of entirely revolutionizing the mode of production."[9]

In the communist utopia, therefore, the nation or community, not individuals, classes or elites, would control the means of production. All property would be owned communally and all the output of that community would be shared according to individual needs. All citizens had a stake in the outcome of their common effort. Everyone in the community would work for the common good. No one would pursue selfish interests. The resources of society would be allocated rationally through a planned economy. The system would produce the material abundance required to satisfy the needs of everyone in the nation instead of the needs of a few wealthy capitalists or landlords. Further, since there would be no class distinctions based on ownership and no domination of one group by another, there would be no classes, no class antagonisms and no class conflicts. And, again from Marx:

> "When, in the course of development, class distinctions have disappeared and all production has been concentrated in the hands of a vast association of the whole nation, the public power will lose its political character…If the proletariat, during its contest with the bourgeoisie, is compelled by the force of circumstances to organize itself as a class, and, by means of a revolution, sweep away by force the old conditions of production, then it will, along with these conditions, have swept away the conditions for the existence of class antagonisms and of classes generally, and will thereby have abolished its own supremacy as a class."[10]

And as the economic basis of society changed, man himself would be transformed. In this new classless, communal society, his selfishness and egotism would wither away and become a relic of the past. Human beings would relate to each other in a spirit of co-operation, seeing each other as partners rather than competitors. A true utopian society would be formed.

The problem is that none of these dreams ever became a reality. First, generating material abundance, that is, producing enough output to satisfy the needs of all the people in a communist society, was critical to ending the competing interests that arose in capitalist societies. But this never occurred under the communist system. Nationalization of industry and collectivization of farming were colossal failures that led to huge economic inefficiencies and shortages of everything from food to consumer goods to industrial materials.

Second, gaining control of the state, its factories, its agricultural facilities, its lands, and people required a great and violent struggle. The great mass of people, including former government officials, the nobility, the middle class, and anyone who owned property or had an interest in retaining the status quo, clung to the old order. These people were going to lose everything they had. So, if the state was going to impose communal principles on the citizenry and sweep away the institutions that had supported the old way, dramatic and violent change was going to have to occur. In every country that experienced a communist revolution, the state had to use terror, purges, trials, imprisonment in vast labor camps, and mass killings to compel people to accept communist restructuring, nationalization, and change. This violence and compulsion led to a more massive alienation of the people than ever occurred under the prior regimes that controlled these countries.

Third, egoism and selfish interest was not eliminated by economic reorganization of society because once mankind's basic needs were satisfied, new ones inevitably emerged to take their place. The problem of rising expectations meant that self-seeking and greed did not disappear. Selfishness did not wither away; inequality did not end, and man did not improve.

Thus, communist societies were hardly utopian, a reality most remarkably demonstrated by the leaders themselves, as they quickly eschewed their revolutionary principles and behaved like the monarchs and aristocratic classes from pre-revolutionary times. The leaders sought and acquired the privileges of rank. Especially in the Soviet Union, they moved into the homes of the wealthy; they owned dachas and summer homes; they used fancy limousines for personal use, and they took over the nobility's style of life. They bought food from special well-stocked stores while their people lacked the basics of life. They became like exploiters of the past, appropriating society's wealth for themselves while starving and depriving their people.

Seventy years after the 1917 Russian revolution initiated the global experiment with communism, the whole communist edifice came crashing down in just months. In spite of the significant number of communist programs implemented worldwide, the massive number of projects undertaken to make communism work in each country, the trillions of dollars spent, and the tens of millions of people killed, no utopia was ever achieved.

Communism, although widely followed, was only one of many formulations of utopian political ideals that were popular in the twentieth century. Utopian political ideologies also found frequent expression in leaders' efforts to restore nations to their former greatness.

In such situations, social and political revolutionaries sought to gain power in countries that had experienced substantial decline after a golden age, by exploiting their citizens' longing for a return to the way things once were. The concept held tremendous appeal to countries that had lost their empire, their position of dominance, or their global status. Nazi Germany under Hitler, Japan after the Meji Restoration, Turkey under the Young Turks, and Cambodia under the Khmer Rouge are relevant examples of this theme.

In each of these four cases, the utopian narrative asserted that their country once had experienced a golden age when it controlled substantial territory; its culture flourished; its economy thrived; and its people accomplished great things. The new leaders claimed that their nation's current decline was the fault of outsiders and internal enemies who were undermining their country and preventing it from regaining its former ascendant status. They envisioned a new social order that would create a stronger, more prosperous entity and that would purge the nation of subversive elements; and they inevitably proceeded to expand their borders through military conquest to establish a new empire spanning a much larger territory.

Unfortunately, it is not just nation states that tried and failed to create a utopia on earth. At various times over the last two thousand years, religious movements have seized control of nation states and used the power of the state to exercise total religious control over society. They have, in effect, transformed religious belief systems with an otherworldly, spiritual focus into a political ideology that was very much concerned with temporal power.

To accomplish this goal, religious leaders create theocracies, literally government according to religious principles. The assumption is that God's law, the Church's law, or the high priest's law override mankind's laws and should be the basis by which societies are run. Their legitimacy is based on their claims about their religion's sacred texts or their prophets' pronouncements, both of which are asserted to be the directly revealed word of God and therefore inerrant.

Instead of a secular society with secular goals and belief systems, a theocracy is run as a religious society with religious goals and religious belief systems. However, whether religious or secular, both are concerned with the exercise of power and the control of the state as the entity which manages the direction, operation, and functioning of society.

The ideals behind theocracies are definitely utopian in character. The Christian, Muslim, and Jewish radical religious elites that establish theocracies each imagine that they are God's soldiers, fighting a cosmic battle against evil and Satan and preparing society for the arrival of the End Times. They believe they have to purge society of its corruption and worldliness; and they feel a powerful need to convert as many people as possible to their religion so that all will be pure for the coming of God and the Last Judgment.

The urgency that believers feel about creating a theocracy means that there is zero tolerance for any violation of God's laws or for any dissent from religious principles. Their laws are strict religious laws, which are frequently enforced with draconian and brutal policies. They prescribe everything including dress codes, grooming, religious practice, and who will be educated and what they will be taught. There are significant restrictions on women and what they are allowed to do. They enforce severe blasphemy laws and sometimes impose the death penalty for anyone attempting to leave the religion. The use of terror, beatings, public torture, and executions are commonplace and are employed explicitly to create fear among the populace and keep everyone in line.

Theocratic forms of government, with the characteristics described above, have recurred frequently across history and continue today. Many Muslim majority countries, including Iran, Saudi Arabia, Sudan, Yemen, Mauritania, and Afghanistan, are run as theocracies. All these theocracies ultimately become dictatorships where people's rights are limited and the religious control society, determine its laws, and use the resources of the state to fund their activities. These are among the worst kind of absolute dictatorships. They are brutal, uncompromising, and prepared to use extreme violence to enforce their ideological principles.

The problem for utopian ideologies, whether religious or political, is that their great ideals and great goals consistently overpower reality, reason, and sanity. The utopian outcomes, which are intensely desired, become primary and more important than all other considerations. This idealism drives many utopian religious and political ideologies to embrace extreme methods to accomplish their goals. The Inquisition, the Crusades, the Killing Fields, the Gulag, the Chinese Great Leap Forward, the Chinese Cultural Revolution, Stalin's and Mao's forced purges and famines, the Religious Wars in sixteenth and seventeenth century Europe, and the Turkish slaughter of the Armenians, are but a few of the terrible consequences that have resulted from mankind's effort to achieve the ideal in this life.

Unfortunately, there are no great success stories that would justify such disastrous results. Mankind's attempts to create and implement utopian societies have never been worth the cost, because no utopian scheme, whether political or religious, has ever led to a utopian outcome, on either a large or small scale.

Given the poor track record of utopian ideas and programs, how can we continue to believe that humanity can ever build a truly utopian world? It seems that there are several issues that are getting in the way of mankind achieving a utopian society in this world:

First, it is unlikely that people will ever be able to come to an agreement on what a truly utopian world would look like. It is and has always been very difficult, given the substantial differences that exist between humans, to come to terms on this issue. People's values, personal characteristics, cultural attitudes, life expectations, life experiences, interests, personal preferences, religious beliefs, and political leanings are among a few of the things that differ, often substantially, from one person to another.

How one person or group of people would describe the perfect world will vary radically from one person to the next and from one society to the next. People are not uniform in their need for security and their tolerance of risk, their degree of motivation, their interpersonal needs, and their tolerance for authority. Some require lots of security, while others need to take lots of risk. Some are looking for others to take charge of their lives, while others are ferociously independent and will tolerate no interference. Some people love to work and be busy, while others like to relax and take it easy. Some like the company of others, while others do not.

Everyone will make different choices based on their genetic makeup, their family background, the environment in which they live, and their ideological preferences. One person's idea of the ideal life and another's are inevitably going to be quite different. Utopian uniformity would seem to be virtually impossible to achieve in most earthly communities, especially given the enormous differences in human beings. Attempting to force fit people into someone's idea of the perfect world has never worked and never will.

The second issue is whether a utopian or perfect society or life is even possible. As we have demonstrated throughout this chapter, mankind's attempts to create the perfect world on this earth have, throughout history, either failed outright or have resulted in disastrous consequences for hundreds of millions of people. Even when religious leaders and holy men have eschewed the idea of building a perfect society and instead tried to focus on living by their own personal ideals of perfection, they have failed miserably. The Catholic priest sex scandals have demonstrated the tremendous fallibility of utopian ideals, like lifetime sexual abstinence. The Buddha's early failures in his attempts to reach Nirvana through ultra-rigid discipline, extreme sacrifice, and a relentless drive for perfection, did not allow him to achieve Nirvana. Instead, it turned out that only a more moderate course of action achieved the desired results. Perfection is a wonderful goal, but it always has unintended consequences that make it unachievable or very deadly.

The third issue is that utopians believe suffering can be eliminated from this life. The reality is that even the best life is full of personal suffering. No one escapes the sorrow and pain of this life. Humans cannot avoid suffering because their own flaws, attachments, unrestrained needs, and unrealistic expectations drive the pain they experience. Their greed for money and possessions, their drive for power over others, their lusts, their ego and narcissism, their predilection for violence, and their thirst for revenge all contribute to their own suffering and that of others. Everyone needs to deal with the reality that suffering is inherent in the human condition and learn how to adjust to this idea. As much as we wish it were different, there is no easy way out, no escape from suffering.

The fourth issue is that any utopian society must be designed so that it fair or just. Most people have the expectation that life's benefits should be distributed equally, either in this world or the next. They also believe that good behavior in this life will be rewarded and that bad behavior will be punished. These ideas are simply not borne out by the facts. The financial and lifestyle rewards of life are highly concentrated among a small handful of people in every country in the world. The top 10% of the population in most countries typically controls 90% of the wealth and most of the political power. They lead very comfortable lives while the masses of people live on the edge of poverty.

What is more, the time and place in which one has lived has historically resulted in radical differences in life conditions and the amount of suffering one experiences. In World War II, those unlucky enough to have lived in Europe, Russia, China, and the Far East, experienced radically different levels of suffering than those who lived in the Western hemisphere, outside a combat zone. Life benefits and suffering have never been and probably never will be equally distributed.

So, if there can be no utopia in this world and this life, maybe there can be a heaven, after we die. Unfortunately, there is no evidence to support the idea that utopias of the next world even exist. The only confirmation comes from ancient texts and revelations whose authoritativeness can be readily challenged. No one has ever seen heaven; no one has ever returned from heaven to report on it. And, as a result, there is no concrete proof of the existence of a heaven or hell. Whether one chooses to believe such things is strictly a personal decision, a matter of faith.

Further, even if one did believe in the idea of a utopian afterlife, the very concept, as described by sacred texts and revelations, is not credible. To the extent that heaven is explained, it is expressed entirely in terms of current human realities. It is a "land of milk and honey," an ideal world where people get all of their earthly desires fulfilled without any of the problems that currently make life so difficult. This is nonsensical. Heaven cannot be the same as earth without the negatives. Heaven cannot be heaven if people go there with the same attitudes, the same needs, the same expectations, the same beliefs, the same longings, the same hatred and anger, the same lusts and cravings that they have on earth. Why? Because we already know the kind of world that this mix of characteristics produces.

The idea of being able to reach paradise in the next life or make this world a more perfect place is extremely alluring, especially given that most people want to experience the ideal in their day-to-day lives. They want their special needs and wishes to be met, whether they are realistic or not. They want people to respect them and recognize their worth, whether they deserve it or not. They expect to be protected from the vagaries of life and relieved of its problems and responsibilities, whether this is realistic or not. They do not want bad things to happen to them. They want whatever good occurs in their lives to last forever and whatever trials they experience to end quickly. They want their world, their society, and their individual lives to get better. But this is not realistic.

The belief that there is an ideal outcome to this life, either in the here and now or in some imagined afterlife, is a primitive and idealistic concept that can never be verified or falsified. It makes people vulnerable to those who seek to manipulate and control them and does little to help them meet the challenges of everyday life. It should be discarded in favor of a more realistic view of life.

Chapter 5

ABSOLUTISM:
THE REFUGE OF SMALL MINDS

Absolutism is the acceptance of and/or belief in absolute principles in political, philosophical ethics.[1] Absolute principles are values or ideas that are held to always be true. They are complete by themselves and do not require any additional thought, evidence, or discussion to be considered valid.

Those who espouse these absolutist principles generally adopt uncompromising positions with regard to the implementation of their beliefs. For example, belief systems, like communism, Christianity, and Islam, have traditionally claimed that their fundamental tenets were ultimate truths that could not be improved upon or surpassed. They declared that theirs was the one and only true faith, above all others. They further maintained that their guiding principles were infallible and unchanging truths. Their legitimacy was derived from what ideologists claimed were unimpeachable sources—divine revelation or inerrant sacred texts in the case of religions or flawless historical analyses in the case of political ideologies. People who refused to acknowledge their infallibility and submit to their dictates have usually suffered severe consequences for their failure to comply.

Further, since absolutists hold that their beliefs are unconditional and come from the highest authority, they will not, by definition, subject their principles to questioning, criticism, alteration or modification. Their positions are so entrenched that they are unable to see any condition that could lead them to different conclusions than the one they have already reached. And, they cannot ever allow doubt, dissent, or debate. For if these things are ever permitted, the proponents of the ideology would be making a tacit admission that their truths are conditional, negotiable, and relative. Given these restraints, absolute beliefs become a self-sealing truth that cannot be penetrated by logic, reason, facts or evidence.

To ensure their standards are met, absolutists impose a rigid set of values, beliefs, and commitments on their followers. They back their standards up with a rigorous code of behavior that must be followed to the letter of the law. Leaders of many religious and political ideologies have historically ensured compliance with their beliefs by aggressively policing, enforcing, and punishing, sometimes in draconian fashion, even the most minute deviations from established orthodoxy. Many Muslim countries, like Iran, Afghanistan, and Saudi Arabia have "morality" police patrolling the streets to do just this job. And many of these same countries have adopted an increasingly aggressive stance about using violence to drive non-Muslims out of their countries to block the presence of alternative beliefs.

But, occasionally, absolute ideologists go even further to prevent any heretical or treasonous practices from creeping into their faith. They create extra-judicial organizations that indict, try, and punish any deviance from established orthodoxy.

In the religious sphere, the Catholic Church used the Spanish Inquisition to eliminate heresy. They set up a special system to investigate, prosecute, and punish those suspected of heretical beliefs. Once targeted, there was no escape; the accused were always guilty. Grotesque tortures were used to extract forced confessions that led to executions and punishments, which were often meted out in public to terrify the average person and remind them of the dangers of not rigorously adhering to Church doctrine.

In the political realm, the Khmer Rouge established a secret prison in Cambodia, the infamous S-21, to root out possible enemies of the regime, specifically those who were suspected of not buying into the prescribed communist ideology. Torture and extreme physical and mental abuse were used to gain confessions of ideological deviance and to help identify other suspected transgressors. Whether the prisoners were actually guilty was never deemed to be important. It was considered perfectly acceptable to kill ten innocent victims to uncover even one case of treasonous belief.

In addition to protecting against heresy and treason, absolutists endeavor to limit their followers' exposure to alternative belief systems. They know that it is difficult to keep their members toeing their ideological line when they can see other people, whether in their town, their country, or the world at large, holding different beliefs and values. Having to confront dissimilar ways of thinking and behaving can be very upsetting to those whose psychological stability depends on ensuring the validity of their own personal worldview. It is very common for absolutists to embrace the idea that the presence of alternative ideologies in their society is a significant threat to their way of life. Two examples are instructive:

In China, Communist Party leaders have sought to completely eliminate alternative ideologies that threatened the Party's control and dominance. Several decades ago, they virtually wiped out Buddhism in Tibet, killing monks, destroying monasteries, and outlawing the practice of the religion; twenty years ago, they neutralized the popular Falun Gong movement through a program of imprisonment and ideological conversion; and now, they are in the process of systematically imprisoning, "reeducating", and repressing all Muslims in Xinjiang, China.

In the Middle East, many Muslim majority countries have used a continuous program of threats and violence to systematically drive Christians and other non-Muslims out of the Middle East. The result is that there has been a significant decline in Christian populations throughout the region over the last several decades. In 1910, 13.6% of the Mideast's population was Christian. By 2025, the figure is expected to be just over 3.0%.[2] This same thing happened in Spain five centuries earlier, during the time of the Spanish Inquisition, when Jews and Muslims were targeted for removal, conversion, or death by the Catholic Church.

Unfortunately, the implementation of absolutist ideas, attitudes, and actions are remarkably pervasive in our world. Historically, most human societies have been run as absolute dictatorships, where a small group or elite within society acquired the wealth, power, and military might that enabled it to completely dominate its own people and outsiders as well. As a result, humanity has most typically lived under the control of absolute rulers who have used their power to exploit or enslave others and carry out their own selfish agendas.

Whether those leaders were pharaohs, emperors, kings, high priests, popes, clerics, or dictators, they all behaved the same way. They built their following and established their absolute authority by using brute force and intimidation, by asserting that they ruled under "the mandate of heaven," or by claiming that they were Gods themselves.

Over time, however, the tools for achieving and justifying

total control of society became more sophisticated and more effective. Prospective leaders began to leverage absolutist religious belief systems, like Islam and Christianity, and subsequently political belief systems, like communism and fascism, as the primary vehicles for attracting and retaining potential followers. When combined with aggressive enforcement tools, like the threat of eternal damnation, torture, purges, executions, and prolonged imprisonment, these ideologies gave them the ability to attract and control large groups of people very efficiently.

As a result of the success of these powerful ideas, the firm grip that absolutists had over society took a long time to erode. The idea that ordinary men would dare confront the absolute political and religious authorities that dominated the world was not even considered a possibility until well into the modern era. The initial challenges to autocracy began in Europe, first in the secular sphere during the Renaissance in the 1400's, then in the religious sphere during the Reformation in the 1500's, and finally across multiple European societies during the Enlightenment in the 1600's and 1700's.

These early revolutionary movements gave people permission to defy traditional authority and limit the power of religious or secular leaders. The idea that states could be governed by leaders elected by the people, rather than absolute rulers, began to spread. Democratic states came into being in England in 1688, in the United States in the 1780's, in France in 1789, and in most of the rest of Europe in 1848. During this period, the belief that people could use reason and intellect to dispute traditional faith or ideologically-based thinking also became increasingly accepted. Autocratic ideologies began to lose credibility in the Western world as they failed to sustain their dominance and fell to more flexible systems.

Gradually, democracy spread to many parts of the world, giving rise to a more open, more moderate, and more fact-based view of the world. Challenging absolutes was acceptable and encouraged. Beliefs had to be proven to be accepted; and the flaws of fixed systems became obvious. The development of the scientific method and the growth of the sciences helped create stunning new advances and innovations that dramatically improved people's knowledge about how the world worked and raised mankind's standard of living to unparalleled heights. Nations that adopted these new modes of thought and government rapidly surpassed those that clung to old absolutist approaches, creating hope that absolutism would wither away.

PATH TO POWER, ROAD TO RUIN

Unfortunately, in spite of the drift to more open societies and the shift to more democratic forms of government, absolutism and absolute ideas have not disappeared. In fact, over the last two decades, they have been staging a comeback as more countries, even once staunchly democratic societies, are seeing constitutional rights eroded or even eliminated. Almost forty percent of people worldwide now live in a country characterized by Freedom House as "not free."[3]

There are many countries, both large and small, including China, Russia, Saudi Arabia, Iran, Syria, Sudan, North Korea, Afghanistan, and Venezuela, that are ruled by absolute dictators, religious authorities, or elites that completely dominate society and suppress freedom of expression and independent thought and behavior. These autocrats are exerting their substantial influence over larger and larger numbers of people worldwide and, at the same time, they are increasing the degree of control and repression they are exercising over their citizens.

There are several reasons why ordinary people, leaders, and ideologues might support this trend and favor fixed versus flexible belief frameworks and systems of government:

People embrace absolute principles, both from their natural human desire to establish certainty and structure in their lives, but also from their need to avoid their opposite—uncertainty and doubt. Uncertainty is an intolerable condition for most humans. Such feelings drive them to act quickly to resolve their discomfort by establishing a set of certainties they can rely on. Social psychologist John Jost's research, discussed earlier, supports these claims:

> "Uncertainty management models assume that people have a fundamental need to feel certain about their world and their place within it, that uncertainty can be threatening, and that people generally feel a need either to eliminate uncertainty or to find some way to make it tolerable and cognitively manageable."[4]

These feelings about certainty and uncertainty drive many people to gravitate toward more rigid, absolutist systems that provide the structure and stability that they consider essential for managing the extreme stresses of their day-to-day lives. They want to believe that there is someone, a benevolent God, a supreme religious leader, or human strongman, who will always be watching over them--providing the structure, order, stability, and safety they need to survive.

Having such firm convictions gives people the confidence

they need to help them deal both with their self-doubts and the very uncomfortable feeling of not knowing for sure whether they have the right answers to fundamental life questions. To achieve certainty, people must become convinced that their beliefs are beyond the possibility of doubt, free from error, and absolutely correct. If beliefs aren't absolute, then people won't believe the leaders can provide the certainty they think is critical to their survival.

The idea that people have such a strong need for certainty and such a great fear of uncertainty is consistent with social psychology research. Uncertainty, and the doubts and fears that go with it, are a crushing burden that many people want lifted from their shoulders as fast as possible. They feel impelled to quickly resolve the ambiguities in their lives by seeking certainties they can grab hold of. People want a predictable, controllable, and safe world in which to conduct their lives.

Leaders and ideologues know this and push people to accept absolute belief systems, either religious or political, to relieve their doubts. People seek absolute beliefs that are definitive and authoritative and that draw credibility from supposedly unimpeachable sources. The greater the claims of infallibility, the more absolute the positions taken, the more rigid the beliefs embraced, and the more dominant the authority figures controlling society, the more uncertainty-averse people like it. They want certainty, even if it is manufactured.

Inflexible, absolutist ideologies provide these people a set of certainties about themselves as individuals and as members of a larger community. They give them a feeling of safety in the face of the dangers and threats posed by their own behavior and that of the society in which they live. They provide a rationalization of their beliefs and give them the confidence they are on the right track. Jessica Stern, an expert in terrorism and its drivers, buttresses this line of thinking in her book, *Terror in the Name of God*:

> "Strict religious communities simplify life by proclaiming an exclusive truth--a closed, comprehensive, and eternal doctrine that provides answers to life's most troubling questions. Rigid rules and severe punishment for transgressors, and clarity are appealing. Modernity creates confusions and fear because it provides too much choice, which can be overwhelming and frightening. Some people crave discipline imposed from the outside and crave closing off options."[5]

This love of imposed order leads people to follow and worship even brutal, totalitarian leaders, like Stalin, Lenin, and Hitler, often long after they are dead. They do so because they revere strong authority figures whom they think provide order and stability in their lives. With this type of structure, there is no longer any need for them to make tough choices, to bear responsibility for their lives, to worry about whether they are doing the right things, or to ask any more questions about why they are here. This is a great relief to most ordinary people and makes them very receptive to the appeals of absolutist leaders.

The ease with which people are willing to buy into absolute belief systems and accept totalitarian rulers makes such ideas attractive tools for prospective and existing rulers to gain and hold onto large groups of dedicated followers. This reality, as surprising as it is, enables leaders to more easily acquire unobstructed control of society and facilitate rapid realization of their personal goals, without having to be subjected to endless discussions to gain buy-in to their ideas.

If an absolute leader wants things done his way and wishes to implement his own agenda quickly, he will generally be unwilling to have to fight with the opposition, argue points of view, be tied up in endless negotiation, or have to face rebellious subjects. By proclaiming his authority as absolute, centralizing control under his leadership, eliminating all obstacles to his will, and avoiding accountability for his actions, there should be few barriers to his achieving his objectives.

As a result, many absolute governments have demonstrated the capability, in the short-term, to accomplish great feats of progress because they do not have to tolerate the interference of legislative bodies and rival groups or go through endless debates about how to proceed with any program. Absolute leaders can direct all the resources of the country to maximize economic progress and direct investments to the highest priority areas. Two examples from Chinese history illustrate how this has worked in the past.

In Ancient China, in the third century BCE, the country was riven by constant warfare among local warlords, each with their own territory. However, a single warlord, Qin Shi Huang, conquered the squabbling warlords and merged their fiefdoms into a single state, free of the constant fighting and bloodshed that had existed before he centralized power. His dictatorial reign allowed China to grow and advance as a single nation, build the earliest section of the Great Wall, and improve the performance of the economy.

The same type of dynamic is occurring again in modern day

China, as Xi Jinping has consolidated all political and military power under his rule and effectively made himself ruler for life. He has allocated the state's resources to establish China as leader in key global technologies, to develop a military that can fight and win wars, to sustain high levels of growth, and to implement his social and behavioral models for the Chinese people. Absolute control is enabling his vision by removing all obstacles and eliminating any need he might have to get others' approval for anything he thinks he needs to accomplish.

But, it is not just authoritarian rulers that seek to establish highly structured, fixed belief systems that are rigid, dogmatic, and uncompromising. The ideologues that build the philosophical framework for the rulers favor this approach as well. They know, from history, that some of the most successful ideological groups, like the Roman Catholic Church and the Communist Party under Lenin and Stalin, were those that explicitly codified their beliefs while eliminating competing and alternative views. In their minds, diversity of views could only lead to chaos, needless and destructive questioning, and endless debate.

Ideologists demand absolute beliefs to prevent pollution of their ideas and silence doctrinal variations that undermine their authority. For example, in the early years of the Mormon Church, personal revelation was allowed as a valid form of knowing the truth about the religion. However, Mormon leaders found that, left unchecked, a doctrine allowing every individual to espouse his own individual revelations began to lead to chaos. The policy led to the development of multiple versions of the religion and a lack of ideological discipline. Eventually, the leaders had to limit personal revelation to only the head of the Church to prevent the existence of unlimited alternative versions of the religion and unlimited moral and behavioral options.[6] Given a choice, absolute ideologues will always gravitate toward fixed, inflexible belief systems which limit followers' choices and keep them under control.

It is clear from the above that, over time, many different constituencies have chosen to embrace absolutist solutions to life problems. Absolute approaches may provide short-term benefits for select people and groups. But, in general, they have not proven to be sustainable or broadly beneficial.

The problem is that absolute truth claims, by their own definition, require a very high degree of certainty--a level of certainty that simply does not exist in the real world. When people claim that a value or principle is an absolute truth, they are saying that it is perfect, that it is always true or valid, and that it has no restrictions, exceptions or qualifications. To qualify as an absolute, it must be a certainty—undeniable, guaranteed, assured, and completely lacking in any doubt. But is there really any such thing as certainty or absolute truth?

Experts who have studied certainty in their professional lives are convinced it does not exist. Dr. Robert Burton, a respected neuroscientist, has concluded, after extensive analysis of case histories, that certainty and other states of knowing emerge spontaneously from our brains without our conscious awareness, without real knowledge to support them, and without any rational assessment as to their accuracy. In his book, *On Being Certain*, he says:

> "Despite knowing how certainty feels, it is neither a conscious choice nor even a thought process. Certainty and similar states of knowing what we know arise out of involuntary brain mechanisms, which, like love and anger, function independently of reason. They are not preceded by conscious thoughts."[7]

Dr. Burton further concludes that feelings of certainty do not provide the basis for establishing an absolutist stance:

> "We need to recognize that feelings of certainty and conviction are involuntary mental sensations, not logical conclusions. Intuitions, gut feelings, and hunches are neither right nor wrong but tentative ideas that must be submitted to empirical testing. If such testing isn't possible, then we must accept that any absolute stance is merely a personal vision, not a statement of fact."[8]

Thus, any thought that emerges spontaneously from our brains has to be viewed with great skepticism and subjected to the same form of empirical testing that anyone would deploy to solve any important business, scientific, or social problem. Failing that, we have to accept that we are dealing with an opinion or thought, not something that rises to the standard required for it to be an absolute.

The interesting thing is that lots of very well-respected and famous people, from all walks of life, share Dr. Burton's conclusions about certainty.

John Stuart Mill, a 19th century political economist, philosopher, member of the British Parliament, and prolific author, claimed in his book, *On Liberty,* that there was "no such thing as absolute certainty, but there is assurance sufficient for the purposes of human life."[9]

Carl Sagan declared in *The Demon Haunted World: Science as a Candle in the Dark*, "Humans crave absolute certainty; they may aspire to it; they may pretend…to have attained it. But the history of science—by far the most successful claim to knowledge accessible to humans—teaches that the most we can hope for is successive improvement in our understanding, learning from our mistakes, an asymptotic approach to the universe, but with the proviso that absolute certainty will always elude us."[10]

Carlo Rovelli, theoretical physicist and author, declared in his book, *Anaximander and the Birth of Science* that "The essence of scientific knowledge is the capacity to avoid clinging to certainties and received worldviews, and instead be prepared to change these repeatedly if need be, in light of our knowledge, observations, and criticisms."[11]

Physicist and Nobel Laureate, Richard Feynman, from the lecture, *What is and What Should be the Role of Scientific Culture in Modern Society,* given at the Galileo Symposium in Italy, 1964: "We absolutely must leave room for doubt, or there is no progress and no learning…People search for certainty. But, there is no certainty."[12]

Problems with the idea of certainty appear everywhere in our lives. In 2002, The George W. Bush administration told the American people that there were weapons of mass destruction in Iraq and that they represented a severe threat to the security of the United States. The administration was so certain that they were right that they committed billions of dollars and several hundred thousand men to the invasion of Iraq. As is now universally known, they were absolutely wrong. There were no weapons of mass destruction in Iraq and no program to develop any. Further, the war resulted in the deaths of thousands of Americans and hundreds of thousands of Iraqis, the displacement of millions of Iraqi citizens from their homes, and the waste of untold financial resources.

The basic Christian worldview has been widely accepted in a good part of the world for well more than a millennium. It has been sold, by Christian Churches, as a package of certainties that could not be disputed. This worldview reigned supreme until the advent of the Age of Enlightenment, near the end of the seventeenth century, when science began to redefine man's understanding of the world and the universe. Over the last several hundred years, many different disciplines played a part in this revolution. Astronomy debunked the idea that the earth was physically the center of the universe and that the planets were held in place by a deity. Paleontology and geology demonstrated that the earth was not just ten thousand years old as indicated by the Church, but rather it was billions of years old. Medicine proved that disease was caused by germs not by evil spirits or God's wrath. Darwin and others provided convincing evidence that mankind was not spontaneously created, but rather evolved up from primates and other more primitive forms of life, over the entire span of earth's history. And finally, psychotherapy has shown that people could heal themselves and cope with the stresses of life without resorting to prayer or divine intervention as the only solution to life problems. These findings were fundamental blows to all "religions of the book" and to their claimed certainty.

Even with the validity of the Christian worldview in doubt, Christian leaders did not abandon their story. Instead, they devised a strategy to re-establish the certainty of their doctrines. This led them to declare that, scientific evidence to the contrary, Christianity's worldview was intact. Their confidence was based on the idea that, while most beliefs sourced from or through humans may indeed be flawed, there is one set of beliefs that could be absolutely true, namely, those supposedly revealed to mankind by an omniscient supreme being. By declaring that their beliefs came from God, either through direct transmissions of God's word to his prophets or from reading their sacred texts, the religious felt they had the basis to assert that their beliefs were inerrant, unchallengeable, and, therefore, absolutely true. Unfortunately for them, careful analysis of the texts suggested that the religious claims did not hold water.

First, in order to be able to declare that the sacred texts were a direct transmission from Jesus or Mohammed, the texts authors' lives would have had to be contemporaneous with those of the prophets. In fact, this is not the case. For example, there was a huge gap between the time when Jesus lived and the first New Testament texts were written:

> "Scholars located the various writings of the New Testament at the different times and places over a period of one hundred years, from the letters of Paul in the 50's of the first century, through the writings of the gospels of Mark and Matthew in the 70's and 80's, the Gospels of John and Luke around the turn of the second century and on to the Acts, Letters, and other writings during the first half of the second century, some as late as 140-150 CE."[13]

Second, biblical scholars tell us that are there are no original texts of the New Testament in existence today. The earliest texts that humans possess were written centuries later and could not possibly have represented a direct transmission from God or his prophets.

"We don't have the originals of any of the books of the New Testament. The copies we have were made much later, in most instances, many centuries later."[14]

Third, most texts that we have today have been modified potentially hundreds of thousands of times. In 2005, Bart D. Ehrman, a respected biblical scholar and author, estimated that there were from 200,000 to 400,000 variants of the Bible that were drawn from 5,700 Greek and 10,000 Latin manuscripts known to exist.[15] Further, Bibles are still being modified today and whitewashed by religious organizations and people in religious publishing to get rid of passages that put the texts' message in a bad light in today's world.

Fourth, until the fifteenth century CE, when the printing press was invented, if an individual wanted to make copies of the existing texts, he had to copy them by hand, one word and one page at a time. As would reasonably be expected, such a huge, time-consuming, and tedious task inevitably led to scribes and copyists making many transcription errors. Add to that, the reality that there was nothing to stop scribes from altering passages, on their own, to reflect their own particular bias about what the texts should have said. Since we know, from historical analysis, that these things regularly happened, it is impossible to claim that we are looking at original work.

Fifth, the Bible is full of contradictory statements that directly conflict with each other. In many cases, they say completely opposite things. William Henry Burr has published a book, entitled, *Self-Contradictions of the Bible*, that identifies one hundred forty-four such contradictions, which I have verified by checking his claims against my own Bible.[16] This reality suggests that the Bible had many authors who wrote at different time periods in different places and may not have known what was in the rest of the Bible.

These five realities demonstrate that sacred texts cannot be considered to be unimpeachable sources of the truth. It is not possible for the Bible to be inerrant if it contains dozens of contradictions. Religious leaders cannot claim that the texts are directly transcribed from the mouth of God or his prophets. They cannot assert that the texts are original copies of the word of God. The evidence shows that they are merely constructs created and modified by men over long periods of time. Therefore, humanity cannot fall back on beliefs in divine revelation and textual inerrancy to establish the authoritativeness of their beliefs that have already been disproven by other means. Again, the claimed certainty does not exist.

It is important to remember that it is not just religious leaders and ideologues that seek to shore up the certainty of their absolutist positions with false and misleading claims. Political ideologues do exactly the same thing. A popular method of establishing the absolute authority for an ideological position is to cite history as the basis for absolutist claims. It is common for leaders to conduct an extensive analysis of their nation's history to show that there is a strong historical basis for any position they choose to take. Earlier, we discussed recent examples of false narratives presented by world leaders, including Vladimir Putin and Xi Jinping. In both these cases, and in all others like them, the historical analyses were contrived, missing critical information, and manipulated to make a point rather than designed to establish the objective reality of a situation.

And, there is yet another reason why absolutist belief positions cannot be considered to be ultimate truths, as is often claimed. The reality is that mankind's belief formation and acquisition processes are fundamentally flawed. Our thinking processes are too weak, too undisciplined, too limited to ever produce absolute beliefs. Absolute belief positions cannot be unconditionally true or certain, given the general unreliability of the sources from which those beliefs are obtained.

Beliefs are generally acquired from a multitude of sources, few of which are reliable or produce beliefs that could ever rise to the level of absolute truths. Three of the most prevalent sources are those that flow from the mental processes of the human mind, those that are acquired from other people, and those that are obtained by blindly accepting the dictates of supposedly unimpeachable sources

We know that a significant number of human beliefs evolve from undisciplined, mental processes in the human brain. Recent books, written by neuroscientists, psychologists, and psychiatrists, such as, Daniel Kahneman, Jonathan Haidt, and Dr. Andrew Newberg, explain how minds develop beliefs. The authors' substantial research challenges three traditional assumptions that people make about the operation of the human brain and its role in the formation of beliefs, i.e., that humans are in control of their own mental processes; that reason plays a crucial role in the development of beliefs; and that an individual's thoughts, impressions, and perceptions offer an accurate assessment of the world. In fact, none of these ideas stands up to scrutiny and scientific analysis.

First, although people have an image of their beliefs being developed through a thoughtfully considered process in their conscious minds, this is not reality. The brain develops beliefs without consent, without people being aware of the mental processes that are going on inside their heads, and without any conscious intervention on their part. Daniel Kahneman, a Nobel Prize Winning economist and psychologist concludes, based on his extensive research, that:

> "You believe you know what goes on in your mind, which [you think] consists of conscious thoughts leading in an orderly way, one to another. But that is not the only way the mind works, nor indeed is it the typical way. Most impressions and thoughts arise in your conscious experience without your knowing how they got there…The mental work that produces impressions, intuitions, and many decisions goes on in silence in our mind."[17]

Sam Harris, neuroscientist, philosopher, and five-time, best-selling author, reinforces these views:

> "You seem to be an agent acting of your own free will…However, this point of view cannot be reconciled with what we know about the human brain. We are conscious of only a tiny fraction of the information that our brains process in each moment…The truth seems inescapable: I, as the subject of my experience, cannot know what I will next think or do until a thought or intention arises; and thoughts and intentions are caused by physical events and mental stirrings of which I am not aware."[18]

The idea that people do not actively control the creation and processing of their own thoughts may be hard to accept. But, as an experiment, people should just try to silence their own minds. If one sits quietly and lets his/her mind take its own course, it will feed him or her an unending stream of thoughts that he or she does not deliberately will into consciousness. The thoughts and beliefs just appear there without consent. In fact, scientists know that human brains are constantly generating beliefs, drawing on perceptions, impressions, intuitions, emotions, and input from the outside world and passing them on to people's conscious minds without any serious evaluation. And there is little one can do to shut down the unrelenting flow of ideas.

Second, the idea that our beliefs are formed by rational processes does also does not hold up to scrutiny. Social psychologist Jonathan Haidt's research is also supportive of this view:

"Independent reasoned judgment is possible in theory, but rare in practice."[19]

"We make our first judgments rapidly; and we are dreadful at seeking out evidence that might disconfirm those initial judgments."[20]

"The subjects [of the research] made up absurd reasons to justify judgments that they had made on the basis of gut feelings."[21]

It would seem, therefore, that people use their rational thinking capabilities, not to create well thought out beliefs, but rather to justify their spontaneously-generated judgments. The idea that their minds consistently follow a disciplined critical thinking process to arrive at a bulletproof conclusion, with the goal of advancing knowledge and getting to the truth, simply doesn't hold water in most cases. People don't take the time to dig deep on every subject; they don't necessarily see the need to do so; and they may not have the critical thinking skills to carry out the needed analysis anyway.

Third, given the way brain-driven beliefs are developed, it is highly likely that these beliefs will be untrustworthy. It appears that the mind creates its own view about the true nature of the world and its own definition of reality. In his book, *Born To Believe*, Dr. Andrew Newberg, an eminent neuroscientist and author, makes these points very clearly:

"Although we are designed to have beliefs, all beliefs have limitations, and every one of them contains assumptions and inaccuracies concerning the true nature of the world. It is also important to recognize that the memories and beliefs that we have about ourselves are most untrustworthy."[22]

"By the time perceptual information reaches consciousness, each individual has transformed it into something new and unique. This reconstruction of reality is the foundation from which we construct all our beliefs about the world...By recognizing these biases, we can become better thinkers, better researchers, and ultimately better believers."[23]

The research findings on the human mind seriously challenge the traditional assumptions people hold about how human brains work and how they form beliefs. It is obvious that few of the beliefs that come from inside the human brain are ever subjected to the kind of analysis, peer review, and vetting that are required to make sure they are objectively accurate. Most are just opinions, judgments, or faith-based positions that describe how someone feels or needs to feel. They are not likely to be accurate representations of reality. This idea is devastating, not only for one's own beliefs but also for those of others.

Analysis shows that other people are an important source of human beliefs. Dr. Newberg and Dr. Haidt's separate research findings both confirm how important others are to the formation of personal beliefs:

> "Children and adult belief systems are continually being altered by other people's beliefs. We automatically assume that what other people tell us is true, particularly if the idea appeals to our deep-seated fantasies and desires."[24]

> "Although we are not aware of it, we are constantly monitoring and mirroring the behavior of our friends, the language of our parents, and the beliefs of the communities in which we live."[25]

> "Many of us believe that we follow an inner moral compass, but the history of social psychology richly demonstrates that other people exert a powerful force, able to make cruelty seem acceptable and altruism seem embarrassing without giving us any reasons or arguments."[26]

Other people's beliefs come to us in two ways: either they are forcibly imposed on us or they are voluntarily acquired by us. The first type are those than inflicted on us by others who use the threat of force or severe outcomes to inculcate their beliefs. That happens in an autocratic state that violently coerces its citizens to comply with its dictates or in a religious theocracy that uses the threat of eternal damnation or deadly force to control its followers. Whether the imposed beliefs have any validity or not, they are treated as though they are completely without error. No one dares challenge the state's or the church's imposed beliefs because any disagreement is seen as treason or heresy and thus subject to sometimes extreme punishment. Since absolutist approaches to governing are very prevalent throughout the world today, with close to three billion people living in such societies, many people have no choice but to accept the beliefs inflicted on them.

Another major source of imposed beliefs are those inculcated in childhood by parents, teachers, and clergy. Most of these adults have, by virtue of their age, already made strong and often inflexible commitments to a set of beliefs. Since the children they are educating are both impressionable and defenseless against the influence of the important adults in their lives, they have neither the mental resources, nor the life experience, nor the power position to override those adults.

Thus, children's beliefs can only be as good as those of the adult figures that guide them. And since many adults don't form reliable beliefs themselves, the children will, out of necessity, struggle to do any better. Finally, there is a great deal of scientific evidence that suggests that beliefs taught in childhood may be remarkably difficult to overcome; so, once ingrained, they remain entrenched long into adulthood. Ultimately, all children conform to adults' beliefs because of their overriding fear of abandonment, intimidation, and conflict. Dr. Newberg explains how this plays out in our lives.

> "We begin our lives without beliefs, yet our brains come equipped with a natural propensity to believe. For the first few years of existence, we unquestioningly absorb the beliefs of others—parents, teachers, and friends—to help us survive the world. We assume, quite naturally, that what we are told is true and these basic lessons become our foundation for building more sophisticated beliefs and ideals…It takes decades before a child develops the capacity to question these early beliefs, which have been unconsciously imprinted into the memory circuits of the brain. Thus, at the core of our knowledge, we find that we embrace many unconscious assumptions that never have been proven to be true."[27]

The problem is that many, maybe most influencers are going to be unreliable transmitters of belief. Parents, teachers, clergy, and other adults will be passing on their own biases and errors in thinking and reasoning. They may lack any sense of how to think critically; or they may have substantial pre-existing commitments which preclude the formation of accurate beliefs. As a result, they may be poor guides as to what constitutes credible beliefs.

Fortunately, as most people get older, they begin to acquire their own beliefs rather than just being passive recipients of others' beliefs. Their beliefs expand to include a broader range of external sources, which they themselves choose, including political and religious leaders, public figures, celebrities, and, importantly, print, broadcast, and internet media personalities. These people have influence because their prestige and "brand awareness" give them strong credibility. For many people, it is often easier to believe well-known people than to do the hard work to figure out accurate beliefs for themselves. As a result, the authority figures' beliefs and opinions are accepted at face value, regardless of how little research they have invested in forming them. The depth of their expertise and the quality of their reasoning, analysis, and recommendations are never evaluated.

People also acquire the viewpoints of those with whom they associate on a daily basis. They are highly motivated to harmonize their beliefs with those others so that they will be accepted as part of the culture or community in which they live and the social groups to which they belong. Social pressure can become a determining factor in developing and accepting beliefs, because the intense fear of being ostracized and alone makes people reluctant to stray from group ideas, whether they are right or not. This reality, in turn, makes beliefs acquired from others extremely unreliable because it is difficult, if not impossible, to assess the rigor with which the friends and relatives have evaluated those beliefs before accepting them.

If we cannot count on beliefs transmitted from other people and if we cannot trust our minds to produce consistently reliable beliefs, what can we do? Given that we know that beliefs and belief systems can have serious consequences and be life altering, it is critical that we know whether our beliefs are accurate and free from error.

People cannot just believe what they want to believe, what they need to believe, what they were taught to believe, and what the people in their life and community push them to believe. They cannot accept the dictates of parents, teachers, priests, and ministers. They cannot just buy into what leaders, politicians, media pundits, talking heads, and other purported experts tell them. They cannot embrace whatever beliefs make them feel better, reduce their anxieties, or fit with their pre-existing biases and commitments.

Given the reality that the human mind, other people's views, and supposedly divine sources cannot be counted on to deliver solid, fact and evidence-based beliefs, it seems foolish to declare either that absolutes are achievable or that absolute belief systems and absolute truth claims can ever be considered universally reliable.

Absolute positions don't stand the test of time. History shows us innumerable examples of where absolutist beliefs end up being watered down by breakaway groups that split off from the absolutist core. Most political and religious belief systems, including Christianity, Islam, and communism, have indeed fragmented into dozens of ideological sub-groups, each with its own unique beliefs and practices, thus making lie of its original claims of absolute truth. Many of these new sects declare that their own particular version of the belief system was righteous and that all competing ideas were false. This very consistent pattern of ideological fragmentation of absolutist belief systems seriously undermines the whole idea of permanent absolute truths.

The reality is that absolutes run counter to the enormous variability in man, his needs, and his cultural backgrounds. People come from different cultures, different traditions, different religions, different value systems, and different lifestyles. They have different upbringings, different educational backgrounds, different life experiences, and different exposure to alternative systems of thought. They are motivated by different things and have different needs, which in turn can drive radically different perspectives about the world and human values and beliefs. As a result, they are likely to hold different views on most major issues affecting humanity. And they will inevitably come to different conclusions about what constitutes knowledge and what represents the truth.

After ten thousand years of civilization, people have been able to find few things that everyone, everywhere, across all cultures, can agree to. Each culture, religion, nation, and ethnic group seems to require its own individual approach to acquiring wisdom and enlightenment. So, the idea that there is one absolute truth, one ultimate answer, or one single pre-packaged moral or political solution that works for all of mankind is just not reasonable.

Further, an additional problem that has cropped up in recent times, is the tendency in a post-modern world, beset by cultural relativism, to view all beliefs as equally acceptable. In an effort to respect peoples' differences and the righteousness of their beliefs, they often put aside the question of validity and allow many types of beliefs to stand unchallenged, whether or not they are derived in a disciplined fashion and properly substantiated.

But the reality is that not all beliefs should have equal standing. Some are consistent with objective truth; and some are not. Some are right; and some are wrong. While many people may recoil at the idea that their cherished beliefs may not be empirically accurate, they have to remember that many of mankind's most widely held beliefs, including ideas that men have sacrificed their lives for, have ultimately been proven to be utterly without merit and subsequently discarded.

Thus, the very idea of absolute answers is meaningless in an ever-changing, highly diverse world. Rather than try to assert and defend absolutist positions in any domain of knowledge, we have to recognize that there is little evidence that supports the existence, use, and validity of absolute positions. Instead, all our knowledge should be couched in the language of probabilities. Any claim we make should evaluated on a continuum from highly likely to probable to possible to highly unlikely, reflecting the enormous uncertainty associated with all human and even scientific assertions. In this way, we are likely to come up with more well-grounded, realistic beliefs and not fall prey to the falsehoods peddled by ideologists.

Chapter 6

SUPREMACISM: RAISING OURSELVES AND LOWERING OTHERS

Supremacism occurs when one particular group of people feels that they are superior to others and, therefore, have the right to dominate, control, and exploit those weaker others. In its essence, supremacism is about comparing and contrasting one group to all the others to establish their relative ranking. Supremacists accomplish this task by attributing either positive or negative characteristics to the competing groups in their society, as the basis for making judgments about them, and assigning them a specific place or rank in that milieu.

Because the world has been divided into an almost limitless number of groups that are competing for position and, ultimately dominance, supremacist ideas have been pervasive over the entire span of human history. People classified themselves and others according to gender, race, ethnicity, skin color, tribal affiliation, nationality, religion, political beliefs, and endless other distinctions. While most of these classifications were arbitrary, people generally attach a great deal of importance to them, using them to enhance their own group's identity and to debase people from competing groups.

Since there are so many groups competing for influence and control, supremacism is now and has always been a ubiquitous and formidable force throughout history. It is pervasive and widely accepted in all places, in all eras, and among all peoples. Its universal appeal has been driven by humanity's powerful ego and self-esteem needs, by peoples' driving desire to define themselves as special, and by their strong tendency to view everyone, outside of their own narrowly defined group, as inferior and possibly dangerous.

Because all groups and all individuals must ultimately compete with others to survive, they have learned that they had to focus on differentiating themselves. They know that, if they are going to win the contest for dominance, or even basic viability, they need to convince themselves and their prospective followers, using all means possible, that they are better than others and that they deserve a favored position in societal hierarchies.

Supremacist ideas have found their expression in some of history's most widely accepted political ideologies, including nationalism, imperialism, racism, and National Socialism. They show up at all levels of the social order, regardless of whether one is talking about the human species in its entirety, the religious and political groups into which mankind divides itself, the hierarchies that establish humans' relative status in society, or the way individual people define themselves and their standing in their own personal milieu.

Supremacism is endemic to mankind. It is wired into our beliefs and views of ourselves and others. It helps sustain our self-esteem and address our fears and anxieties about our relations and our standing with others. Establishing individual or group superiority is a fundamental need for most humans. We do this in a variety of ways.

We create narratives that allow us to position mankind as inherently better than the rest of God's creation. For example, people have consistently asserted that we humans are the most advanced form of life to be found in the known universe. The Bible claims that people were made in the image and likeness of God, that nature was meant to be subservient to men, and that humans were chosen to rule over all other species. From Genesis:

> "Let us make man in our image, after our likeness; and let them have dominion over the fish of the sea, over the fowl of the air, over the cattle, and over all the earth, and every living thing that creeps on the earth."[1]

This notion of universal superiority finds further expression in peoples' beliefs, up through the sixteenth century and beyond, i.e., that our solar system was the center of the known universe and that all the stars and the sun revolved around the Earth. Even today, many religionists believe so firmly in humanity's centrality in the universe that they assert that their omniscient, omnipotent, and omnipresent God spends all his time attending to individual people's daily needs, wishes

PATH TO POWER, ROAD TO RUIN

and prayers, and has even prepared a paradise in the next world for those people who live worthy lives.

In other words, people believed that God made our vast universe, spanning trillions of light years and encompassing a virtually limitless number of galaxies and suns, for one species, mankind. The idea that humanity is the elite of creation and superior to everything else in the universe, is a remarkable, but widely accepted conceit.

Such supremacist attitudes are not just pervasive at the species level, but also at the level of human groups. Almost every imagined aggregation of humanity—whether nation state, ethnic group, race, or religion—has, at one time or another, defined itself as the height of human evolution—the culmination of centuries of struggle, conflict, and social development.

All these groups believed they were privileged among all peoples and entitled to a special position in the world. They all buttressed their assertions of superiority with special identity and legitimacy claims.

Virtually every monotheistic religion has claimed that it was the one true religion, that God has forged a powerful covenant with its believers, and that only its own committed adherents would enjoy God's blessings in heaven. For example:

The Jews believed they had a special relationship with God, by virtue of a covenant established with Abraham early in Israel's history. From the Hebrew Bible:

"And I will make thee a great nation; and I will bless thee and make thy name great; and thou shalt be a blessing."[2]

"For thou are a holy people unto the Lord thy God. The Lord thy God hath chosen thee to be a special people unto himself, above all people that are upon the face of the earth."[3]

Christianity made similar claims. The Apostle Paul asserted that Christians had replaced the Jews as God's Chosen People and the world's pre-eminent religion. Paul was the first to make the link from God's covenant with Abraham through to Jesus, the Messiah. By sending his only begotten Son to save mankind, Paul claimed that God had forged a new covenant with Christians by virtue of their belief in Jesus as Messiah. Jews who did not convert to Christianity were no longer part of the sacred covenant. In Galatians, Paul said:

"There is neither Jew nor Greek, there is neither bond nor free, there is neither male nor female: for ye are all one in Christ Jesus. And if ye be Christ's, then are ye Abraham's seed, and heirs according to the promise."[4]

Most Muslims hold similar beliefs and claim that their prophet, Mohammed, was chosen to receive God's message from the archangel Gabriel. They declare that their sacred text, the Koran, is the one true and final revelation from God. They further assert that both the Jewish Old Testament and the Christian New Testament, which preceded the Koran, were also originally true. But their texts were altered and corrupted by the leaders of their religions. As a result, their followers were led astray and no longer knew the true message of God. Therefore, in the minds of Muslims, Islam had taken the place of Christianity and Judaism as the paramount world religion above all others.[5]

Religions are not alone in adopting a stance of ascendancy for themselves. Nation States also tried to assert their supremacy over other nations and peoples. Nineteenth and twentieth century imperialists, from England, France, Spain, Portugal, Belgium and Germany, proclaimed that white Europeans had been chosen by historical circumstances to lead the people of less developed countries into the modern world. In the view of the imperialists, one only needed to look at the huge advantage that European nations held over the rest of the world in relative economic, technological, and cultural spheres to realize that Europeans were superior and destined to lead others. It was the burden of white men to shepherd the development of the lesser peoples since they were not capable of governing themselves in a civilized way. The imperialists' goals were: to maximize the colony's land, resources, and economy, to get the natives to embrace a more sophisticated cosmology about the true nature of the universe, and to persuade them to accept Christianity.

Also, Nazi Germany, representing an extreme version of supremacism, positioned itself and the Aryan people at the top of the evolutionary ladder. Hitler wrote that Aryans had emerged from centuries of struggle and conflict as above all other races. They were the culmination of a prolonged process of historical evolution and Darwinian struggles, leading to their position as the "Master Race." He argued that there should be no interbreeding between Germanic peoples and the degenerate races of Eastern Europe, especially the Slavs, the Jews, and the Gypsies. If this happened, it would pollute the purity and superiority of the Aryan bloodline. To protect the sanctity of this bloodline, he

　　　　PATH TO POWER, ROAD TO RUIN

proposed that the inferior races should be driven beyond the borders of Germany, enslaved, and/or eliminated.

Like the Nazis, the dominant faction in many countries has often divided its society into groups, creating a hierarchy of its people, assigning each group a rank and granting them privileges and power based on that ranking. Societies have been structured internally along hierarchical lines since the beginning of human history. Hierarchies are a ranking of people according to their relative standing or value in society. As James Waller indicates in his book, *Becoming Evil*:

> "While humans do not have rigid pecking orders, all of our cultures recognize some kind of social dominance hierarchy in which status, prestige, esteem, honor, respect, and rank are accorded differentially to individuals."[6]

The purpose of such ranking has always been to preserve the supremacy and privilege of the upper echelons, while ensuring that the lower tiers remained compliant and accepting of their inferior status. Isabel Wilkerson, in her much acclaimed book, *Caste*, supported this idea:

> "Any action or structure that seeks to limit, hold back, or put someone in a defined ranking, seeks to keep someone in their place by elevating or denigrating that person on the basis of a perceived category, can be seen as casteism. Casteism is the investment in keeping the hierarchy as it is in order to maintain your own ranking, advantage, privilege, or elevate yourself above others or keep others beneath you."[7]

Hierarchies broadly define how a society will operate, who will be in charge, who will have what roles, who will receive critical resources, who will be favored with special privileges, who will be treated well, and who will not. Unfortunately, the creation of hierarchies has frequently led to the granting of significant privileges and advantages to those in the highest tiers and to the abuse of those on the lower levels of society. Those on top typically attempt to solidify their dominant position by violently or ideologically repressing the groups beneath them, thus ensuring that they never have the opportunity to escape their low station in life.

These ideas have played out over and over gain in history. We have already talked about the case of the American South under the Jim Crow laws and the case of the Caste system in India. We also know that similar ideas and practices occurred in South Africa under apartheid, where the majority black populations was rigidly controlled by the minority white regime.

Communist societies also created hierarchies, based on a citizen's loyalties to the communist cause and its leaders. For example, Barbara Demick, in her book about North Korea, *Nothing to Envy*, described how Kim Il Sung, the leader of North Korea, decided in 1958 to undertake a massive project to classify his people into more than fifty different groups. Every person in the country was put through a significant number of background checks in order to give each a ranking as to their estimated political reliability. Kim Il Sung and his family were ranked at the top of the societal pyramid, along with his close associates and people with impeccable revolutionary credentials. At the bottom of the hierarchy were those who were, by virtue of their previous associations and history, considered politically suspect, e.g., "families of wealthy farmers, merchants, industrialists, landowners, those whose private assets had been completely confiscated, pro-Japan and pro-US people, reactionary bureaucrats, defectors from the South...Buddhists, Catholics, expelled public officials, and anyone who helped South Korea during the Korean war."[8]

People of lower rank were banned from living in Pyongyang and the warmer, more fertile parts of the country. They had no hope of ever advancing their political or economic position because their low status was unchangeable. This type of structured hierarchy was not new to Korea which had, in the past, been bound by a caste system as restrictive as the one in India. "The old class structure relied heavily on the teachings of the Chinese philosopher, Confucius, who believed humans fit strictly into a social pyramid."[9]

Feudal society in Europe was, for centuries, also strictly organized along hierarchical lines, starting with the King, and then moving down the line to the nobles, the knights, and the peasants. Each of these groups had its specific rights, consistent with its position in the hierarchy, and specific obligations to the levels immediately above it in society. Those at the bottom of the hierarchy were locked in for life. They could not advance their station or leave their land without the express permission of their nobles. They were bound by what Peter Singer calls "an authoritarian religion, and a morality based on concepts of loyalty, obedience, and fulfilling the duties of one's station in life."[10]

In this condition, the feudal serfs shared the same fate as their counterparts in Russia and in the Far East. They also lived in a hierarchical pecking order that consigned them to the lowest rungs of society and exploited them ruthlessly. These systems were held in place by what amounted to totalitarian religions that required total submission to the pre-ordained societal structures created in feudal times.

Finally, we are all aware of the long sad history of the suppression of women and the limitations placed on their roles in virtually all societies around the globe. Perhaps, this idea was, at one time, justified by the need to have women focus on producing and caring for children when the survival of our species was a real issue. However, such rigid gender roles are no longer necessary as the world is adequately populated, and possibly overpopulated. Further, since there are so many more childcare options available, women now have the chance to express their rights and assert themselves as independent individuals. Today, the limitations placed on women have become an anachronism, sustained by men who are desperately trying to protect their traditionally dominant role by all means possible. A strong statement of their case is that:

> "Male supremacists view women as genetically inferior, manipulative and stupid. Many male supremacists reduce women to their reproductive function – simultaneously shaming women for having sex while believing that sex is something women owe men or that should even be coerced out of them. Adherents of this ideology are fixated on rigid gender roles and vilify any deviation from their strict gender dichotomy, seamlessly weaving together misogyny, transphobia and homophobia."[11]

It is noteworthy that each of the five hierarchical systems, discussed above, was justified/sustained by political and religious ideologies, specifically: white male supremacism in the treatment of African Americans and women; Hinduism in the case of India's Caste System; communism in the stratification of North Korea; and Christianity as the protector of the feudal system in Europe. It appears then, to quote Evelin Lindner, social scientist and author of the book, *Making Enemies*:

> "There is nothing automatic about how the vertical scale operates to rank human beings. It is not a natural law, like gravity. The vertical scale's use on human worthiness is purely ideological, dependent on the world view or philosophy that individuals and cultures construct for its expression."[12]

This is an important insight. As we can see from the examples above, ideology can and does play a critical role in determining the relative standing of people in many, and perhaps most, societies. Supremacist positions are, in effect, legislated by leaders with a vested interest in establishing or retaining a certain order or structure in society. Ideologies can create and legitimize these hierarchical positions, sustaining and justifying them, and keeping them in place at the expense of those on the bottom rungs of the social ladder. When a hierarchy is rationalized by a belief system, it is very hard to ever escape or migrate to a higher level. Supremacist positions become locked in to ensure that those on top get to maintain their superior view of themselves indefinitely.

So where does all this focus on supremacism come from? The wide-ranging existence of supremacism at the hierarchical, group, and species levels stems from every human's endless individual quest to be better than others. Humans constantly seek, throughout their lives, to construct an individual self-image that makes them feel unique, proud of themselves, and superior to those around them. People achieve a strong self-image in a variety of different ways. Some people have the personal qualities, motivation, work ethic, and temperament that readily leads them to outperform and distinguish themselves relative to their peers. James Marcia's work on identity development characterizes this most advanced state of identity achievement in the following manner:

> "You have reached identity achievement, having a firm and relatively secure sense of who you are. You have made conscious and purposeful commitments to your occupation, religion, beliefs about sex roles, and the like. You have considered a wide range of views, beliefs, and values held by others in achieving this identity, but you have branched out to achieve your own resolution."[13]

Most people, however, are not willing to make the investment of effort required to carve out a distinctive identity position for themselves. Instead, they end up borrowing or constructing their self-image in a variety of different ways.

A leading option for building self-esteem has always been to join/belong to a group. According to James Waller:

> "In Tajfel's social identity theory, one tool used by individuals to enhance their self-esteem is identification with specific social groups. By allowing the in-group to become an extension of

ourselves, we open another avenue to enhance our self-esteem."[14]

Groups can boost individual self-worth and self-esteem by making their members feel that they are part of something special. The leaders tell their new recruits either that theirs is the one true religion; that they are part of a great nation with a great history and future; or that they are part of a group with a special mission. People who feel marginalized by society and those who are emerging from significant life crises are most vulnerable to the appeal of these groups and most likely to benefit from them. This is so because identifying with a group can lift people out of their old life, make them feel important by association, and give them a new identity, one that restores their sense of self-worth and causes them to feel special.

Groups can also give members a purpose or mission in life, which can be critical to building self-esteem. Usually, when people join a group, they are expected to participate in its missions--whether that be proselytizing to expand its membership, working on a religious group's social causes, contributing to or volunteering for a political campaign, or carrying out criminal business in the case of a gang or terrorist group. These activities can be fulfilling, exciting, and sometimes dangerous. They build a sense of commitment to the group and make new members feel like they are doing something important, which can fulfill them as people.

Finally, groups can offer new members supportive relationships and friendships. New members are usually flattered, embraced and given a sympathetic ear. They find people with whom they have shared values and a common cause. As a result, they no longer feel isolated or marginalized. Their self-esteem jumps because they have friendships that build self-worth; and they no longer have to feel alone.

A different option for building individual self-esteem, beyond group affiliation, revolves around status concerns. One of the most important factors driving the individual's pursuit of a position of personal superiority is the need for status, defined as an individual's social or professional standing relative to other people. The centrality of status is well-established by research. A December 9, 2020 New York Times article, written by Thomas Edsall, entitled *The Resentment that Never Sleeps*, synthesized the results of the academic studies on status. Edsall concluded that social status concerns are important drivers of human behavior; that status can be as important as money and power for many people; that fear of losing status can create significant anxiety, even more so than the actual loss itself; and that people have a strong need to believe that they are part of a dominant status group.[15]

One way to establish status is for people to manufacture an identity, whether true or not, and market that identity to those around them. Because many people are afraid that they are not truly superior, they work hard to create a picture of themselves that will make them feel special. In the era of social media, this can happen in a number of different ways. Because status is a relative characteristic that is measured in relation to someone else, it is very much an "us vs. them" issue. We can see this human drive for status in white supremacists who fear that they are being replaced by blacks and losing their position in the America's social hierarchy. We can see it in Putin's need to have Russia be the equal of the United States in world affairs.

Those seeking advanced status can use multiple venues, including social gatherings, social networking sites, and personal web sites, to embellish expansively on who they are and what they do. They can use Facebook and other social media posting as a favored tool for identity construction. It allows them to create a glowing, pre-packaged image of themselves and a picture of their daily life that they think will invite envy and make them feel special. They get immediate feedback when their friends click like or dislike after reading their postings. This kind of image building is pervasive in our society; but it requires constant attention because it is hard to sustain an image that is fabricated and demands endless invention.

Alternatively, people can acquire tangible symbols of success to convey an image that others desire or envy. They can drive fancy cars, wear expensive brand name clothes and jewelry, and attend events for the rich and famous. They can attach themselves to celebrities, sports figures, sports teams, and wealthy acquaintances, eat in exclusive restaurants, and join elite clubs. Everywhere they come into contact with others, they are constantly positioning themselves to make others think they are incredibly successful. Every cocktail party or social event is a series of acting and image performances. These symbols then become their identity and enhance their ego and self-worth.

Regardless of how they ultimately choose to build up their identity and fill their intense need to feel special, individuals are inevitably going to consume an enormous amount of lifetime energy catering to their own personal ego, self-esteem, identity, and status needs. Unfortunately, people and groups never find it sufficient to raise themselves up. They only seem to be able to achieve true superiority by employing a dual supremacist strategy of instinctively and repetitively trying to find ways of elevating themselves and lowering all others at the same time. In the process of executing this plan, they became very adept at casting others down, using three tools, i.e., denigration, dehumanization, and demonization.

Of the three types of lowering processes, denigration is definitely the mildest. It begins by belittling people from other groups as a natural consequence of competing for social advantage. It is merely an attempt to establish some basis for superiority without necessarily having any malevolent intent with regard to the targeted people. The denigrator merely wants to satisfy himself that he is better, using special narratives designed to make himself feel better or make others feel worse. It is, however, like a gateway drug that ultimately leads people to a more aggressive stance, either dehumanizing or demonizing them.

Supremacist groups dehumanize members of another group when they assert that the other group is inferior, beneath them, and not worthy of their respect. Dehumanizers claim that the others' appearance, their cognitive abilities, their cultural practices, their behavior, and their beliefs are primitive and below the minimum qualities they need to be seen as human beings.

Dehumanizers feel no obligation to treat those designated as sub-humans according to basic human standards of morality, fairness, and human decency. They think that it is acceptable to deny them any opportunity that would raise their position in life or give them a sense of pride. They feel no restraints about seizing their lands, possessions, and homes. They believe they can freely abuse, terrorize, enslave, suppress, and even eliminate them if that is their desire.

To the supremacist, "others" are little better than animals or disease. In fact, in the runup to genocides, such as the Holocaust or the killing in Rwanda and Cambodia, the perpetrators continuously referred to their victims as bacilli, bacteria, pestilence, vermin, lice, cockroaches, and rodents. Such degradation automatically devalued the victims and made it easier to get fellow citizens to go along with their elimination.

The next level of degradation is demonization. Demonization goes beyond dehumanization, which labels people as barely human or sub-human and says instead that they are demonic, allied with the devil, and the enemy of all that is good. They are irreparably evil, morally corrupt, and dangerous in the extreme. Demonization is an appellation usually reserved for an enemy, who deserves hatred rather than just contempt.

Feelings of hatred arise when people feel threatened and are afraid. People hate when someone endangers loved ones, threatens their economic livelihood, steals/appropriates their property, takes away their rights, or humiliates them. These are all things that beget strong emotional responses, including anger, rage, fear, desire for revenge, and a wish to eliminate the perpetrators. These feelings lead people to move beyond just dehumanizing to the more aggressive stance of demonizing and eliminating them.

In the end, denigration, dehumanization, and demonization are the inescapable and deadly outcomes of dividing society into "us-them" groupings. The question is why humans, whether as individuals or members of groups, have such an intense need to focus so intensely on "us vs. them" distinctions?

The first answer to this question is that humanity has been programmed, after thousands of years of human evolution, to be very wary of strangers or people who are different from themselves. We know that early mankind was, in fact, divided into limitless small tribal groupings that inevitably had to come into conflict with one another. Traveling in small hunter-gatherer groups, they quickly learned to be wary of any outsider who might poach on their hunting grounds or pose a serious threat to their safety. Every stranger brought with him the possibility of death, the kidnapping of women, and the stealing of food and possessions. Therefore, anyone who did not belong to their tribal group had to be treated with extreme caution.

The resulting fear and distrust of others grew with time. It created significant tribal animosities, increasing levels of conflict, and a real "us-them" mentality in humans, so much so that the "us-them" approach to life became instinctive for humanity.

Dr. Robert Sapolsky of Stanford University, in his landmark book, *Behave,* tells us that human brains now distinguish between in-group and out-group members in a fraction of a second and encourage people to be kind to the former but hostile to the latter. Such mental behavior, he says, is automatic, unconscious, often based on minimal actual differences, and develops at astonishingly young ages.

> "The strength of us/theming is shown by: (a) the speed and minimal sensory stimuli required for the brain to process group differences; (b) the unconscious automaticity of such processes;

(c) its presence in other primates and very young humans; and (d) the tendency to group according to arbitrary differences, and then to imbue those markers with power."[16]

These tendencies only strengthen as we get older. We grow to become very entrenched in our attitudes towards others, especially relative to ourselves and our group. Unfortunately, this approach to life can be quite harmful and self-reinforcing.

James Waller teaches us, in his book, *Becoming Evil,* that assigning people to in-groups and out-groups has problematic aftereffects, each of which serves to reinforce polarization and conflict and increase our perception of in-group and out-group differences.

"We perceive other in-group members as more similar to us than to out-group members."[17]

"We see members of the out-group as all alike…If we know something about one out-group member, we are likely to feel that we know something about all of them."[18]

"We amplify the assumed similarity of in-group members and homogeneity of out-group members by drawing ever starker lines between "us" and "them". We draw these lines by exaggerating the differences between our group and the out-group."[19]

"In Tajfel's words, "the mere perception of belonging to two distinct groups… is sufficient to trigger inter-group discrimination favoring the in-group…" We evaluate in-group members more positively, credit them more for their successes, hold them less accountable for their failures or negative actions, reward them more…and find them more persuasive than out-group members."[20]

These four effects are the cognitive mechanisms that make it easy for people to see their own group as superior and other groups as inferior. They also facilitate the process of denigrating others and then taking harsh actions against them. Because we don't see other people as individuals, we don't try to understand their common humanity and bond with them. Instead, we just emphasize differences and intensify the "us-them" dynamics.

Unfortunately, these tendencies are not something many of us leave behind as we get older. It is ingrained behavior and it has real consequences for how we view others and our relationships with them. The strong human bias to fragment into groups and the resulting "us-them" mentality has made conflict between groups inevitable and very dangerous for humanity.

In fact, history has shown us that most of the worst types of human conflict perpetrated in modern history have begun with dehumanizing and/or demonizing a targeted population; most imperialist adventures have been justified by portraying the victims as inferior to the conqueror; most ideologically-based long-term conflicts are fueled by the belief that the enemy is demonic and beyond repair; and most instances of long-term repression have been rationalized by labeling the "other" as primitive, apelike, and incapable of advancement. Supremacist ideas are an integral part of both political ideologies, like nationalism, imperialism, and racism, and religious ideologies, like conservative Islam and Christianity. Some examples include:

Japanese nationalists have, throughout their history, declared that they were superior to all other peoples. They proclaimed that Japan was the 'Land of the Gods," that the Emperor of Japan was divine, and that the Japanese were God's chosen people. For the Japanese, all other races, nationalities, ethnic groups, and religions were beneath them. When they invaded and conquered Korea, China, and most of Southeast Asia, they felt no compunction about brutally slaughtering many millions of people, driving women into sexual slavery, and making people work in forced labor camps.

When the Khmer Rouge overthrew the Cambodian government in 1975, they created clear distinctions between their revolutionary group and everyone else who lived in Cambodia. Anyone who was not designated a true Khmer was considered unworthy to live in their new paradise and was targeted for elimination. Muslims, Chinese, Vietnamese, city dwellers, the bourgeoisie, and members of the former Cambodian government were all considered to be vermin, pests, and people of no significance. As a result, their sole value was as a slave labor resource. Beyond that, they were completely expendable. This attitude led to the murder of two million people in Cambodia during the brief reign of the Khmer Rouge.

Europeans, southern planters, and slave traders justified the African slave trade by asserting that Black Africans were irredeemably inferior, and perhaps not even human. They claimed that the entire African continent was backward. Africans were heathens, bereft of Christianity and godless people without souls. The slave traders claimed that tyranny, war and chaos were the natural condition of the African continent. Because Africa was so barbaric and chaotic, Black Africans were better off as slaves, since slavery saved them from worse fates that would have befallen them had they remained in their homelands. An example of these ludicrous rationalizations was:

> "The purchase of slaves was actually a humanitarian act because the unbought would routinely be slaughtered by their savage African captors. Thus English slavers were saving lives."[21]

With this elaborate justification in place, millions of Black Africans died in the Atlantic slave trade, and probably twice as many died in the Arab slave trade. They were completely expendable.

Thus, groups of all kinds have used supremacist ideas to advance their religious and political agendas and to rationalize the horrific actions they take against those "others." Intergroup conflicts, motivated by the need to establish supremacy over or domination of others, have been behind the killing of millions: in Nazi Germany, six million Jews, gypsies, and other minorities were the victims; in Rwanda and Burundi, Tutsis and Hutus slaughtered each other to keep control of their countries; in Bangladesh, West Pakistani Muslims killed one to two million Hindus and Bengali Muslims to force them to stay part of West Pakistan; and in Turkey, Muslim Turks killed as many as three million Armenian, Greek, and Assyrian Christians to purify their country of non-Muslim influences.

In addition, imperialist adventures and exploitation of weaker others have caused the deaths of tens of millions of people in the Americas, the Far East, Africa, and Latin Americas. Irreconcilable group hatreds have been at the heart of the twentieth century's most prolonged violent conflicts, including the Israel-Palestinian crises, the Pakistani-Indian wars, and the "troubles" in Northern Ireland. And the need to sustain traditional societal hierarchies has meant the sometimes violent oppression of the lower levels of society.

Wherever any group of humans has set itself above and apart from its fellow man, wherever intolerance of differences prevailed, wherever intergroup hatred has boiled over, trouble has followed. Because the price of sustaining and enacting supremacist ideas and policies is so high, we have to ask ourselves whether our inflated opinions of ourselves and negative views of others really have any validity and are worth the costs they impose on humanity.

The problem is that, as a species, we humans are obsessed with dualities. For most of us, the world consists of two camps that are fundamentally in opposition to one another. There are believers and non-believers, God's chosen people and the rest of the world, the citizens of our nation and those of other nations, and the members of our religious, racial or ethnic group and everyone else.

As a result, we live in the world of "us" and "them," where we are superior and everyone else is subordinate. We concentrate on our differences with others, ignoring our many commonalities, and desperately cling to our separate and unique identities. We stress what divides us from others, rather than what unites us. In doing so, we end up making judgments of people, not based on who they are as people, but rather on things that have little to do with whether they can significantly contribute to our society. And, as is shown in the next chapter, there is no evidence, either in history or gene science, to show that any individual or group is sustainably superior to any other, regardless of what we think and how we behave.

Chapter 7

THREE DANGEROUS IDEAS
CURRENTLY IN PLAY

There are three very dangerous, ideology-driven ideas that have been circulating in the United States and around the world in the last few years. They have been the centerpiece of the Republican Party's campaigns for the last three Presidential election cycles and have been used by Donald Trump to gather a significant and very loyal following.

What's more, these ideas are having a disproportionate influence on American politics and are driving and distorting the thinking of significant numbers of people in this country. These thoughts have evolved from utopian, absolutist, and supremacist beliefs that are popular among certain segments of the population, but very dangerous for the future of the country. These ideas have gained credence in our society even though they are not properly grounded in terms of their supporting logic; don't reflect historical realities; and don't consider the consequences that will inevitably emerge when implemented in the real world. If we allow these ideas to undermine American democracy, as they inevitably will, then we will pay a very high price as a nation.

The first of these three dangerous ideas is the very utopian notion that people can restore their nation to its former glory. When an empire collapses or a nation loses some of its status as a regional or world power, the citizens of that country are vulnerable to those who promise to restore their country's former greatness. A mythically once-great people inevitably long to be "great again," to recapture their former glory, and to re-establish what they perceive to be their rightful place in the world. Unfortunately, the conditions that originally led to a nation's early success no longer exist and cannot be easily replicated. This provokes leaders to take extreme positions to achieve what amounts to an impossible goal.

In the first chapter of this book, I mentioned that three of today's most powerful leaders, Vladimir Putin, Xi-Jinping, and Donald Trump have used the lure of making their country great again to implement a strategy of national revitalization and to rationalize a very aggressive stance towards other nations.

For Vladimir Putin, "The break-up of the Soviet Union was the greatest geopolitical disaster in history." Because he believes this so strongly, much of what he has done over the last several years has been designed to reverse that reality and re-establish Russia as a leading global power that can wield significant influence in the world and on the Eurasian continent. In his view, for Russia to be great, it must reverse the loss of its former empire, control all former Russian lands, and win its war against Ukraine.

For Xi Jinping, China was, at one point in its history, a great and powerful nation that was destroyed by invading and exploiting foreign powers, including Japan, Great Britain, and France. These three countries killed its people, stole its resources, and left the country destitute. With the rise of the Chinese Communist Party to power in 1949, China has embarked on a great rejuvenation that has made it an economic powerhouse, with a rapidly expanding military, and a desire to be pre-eminent power on the world stage.

Donald Trump, in America, has adopted a similar line of thinking, asserting that America is in decline, needs to withdraw from its commitments to its allies around the world, deport immigrants and other undesirable populations, support the return of white male supremacism, endorse Christian nationalism, end the regulation and taxation that has been imposed on American business, and adopt a hard line on China. He asserts, without proof, that if we commit to these policies and follow his leadership, America will become great again.

While the outcome of these three efforts is as yet unknown or incomplete, history has provided four excellent examples of the "Restore Former Greatness" approach, from Ottoman Turkey, Nazi Germany, Imperial Japan, and Khmer Rouge Cambodia. Their stories demonstrate clearly what happens when countries go in this direction. It is a very cautionary tale:

Ottoman Turkey: At its peak in the 16th century, the Ottoman Empire extended from Eastern Europe to Iraq to the Arabian Peninsula to parts of Libya, Egypt, and Southern Spain. But, three centuries later, the empire was reduced to the borders of modern-day Turkey by a series of disastrous wars with Russia and the European powers as well as rebellions against Ottoman rule during the 19th and early 20th centuries.

In 1908, the Committee for Union and Progress, also known as the "Young Turks," took over the government of Turkey from the Sultan. Young Turk leaders envisioned reclaiming the Russian Caucasus and central Asia as a path to recreating the Ottoman Empire and establishing a new golden age for the Turkic people. They advocated that Turkey could only be revitalized if it rid itself of its non-Turkic and non-Muslim elements and created a pure homogeneous nation. As part of this program, Turkey targeted the Armenians and the region of Armenia as both a geographic and cultural obstacle to creating a new Ottoman Empire. The problem for the Turks was that the Armenians were Christian, their country lay geographically in the way of Turkey's planned move eastward, and they continued to resist Turkish domination. In the minds of the Young Turks, the Armenians and the Armenian nation needed to be eliminated.

The Turks saw World War I as a way to end all foreign interventions and unite Turkic peoples under a new expanded Ottoman Empire. Turkey abrogated all treaties with Western Europe, including those affecting Armenian rights. Obsessed with their mortal enemy, Russia, and angry about Russian rule of the Turkic peoples of central Asia, the Turks entered the war against Russia in 1914 to create a pan-Turkic state that united all Turkic peoples.

Under the cover of World War I, they embarked on a wholesale slaughter of the Armenian peoples to clear Armenia of non-Turks and non-Muslims. They succeeded in killing approximately two million Armenians, half a million Greeks, and half a million Assyrians, but lost the war with Russia and ended up on the losing side in World War I. The Turkic dreams of a new empire were forever crushed.

Nazi Germany: In the late 19th and early twentieth centuries, the German empire was a force to be reckoned with. It had achieved substantial economic success and created a formidable military power. Unfortunately, it used its military position to ill effect when it started and then lost the First World War. The German surrender to the Allied Powers was a shock to people in Germany, a real blow to the idea that they were a great nation.

Germans did not think the capitulation was warranted and, as a result, felt betrayed by their leadership, especially when they were forced to submit to the will of the Allied Powers that had defeated them and accept the punitive terms of the Versailles Treaty. The Treaty required Germany to give up substantial territory, demilitarize, and pay burdensome reparations, all of which led to a series of debilitating economic crises, currency devaluations, agricultural disasters, staggering unemployment, episodes of violence, and constant changes in leadership.

It was in this environment that Hitler and the Nazi Party rose to power in the 1930's, promising to restore German greatness by nullifying the Versailles Treaty, rebuilding the military, eliminating unemployment, and creating a racial utopia free of foreign influences. Within eight years of assuming power, Hitler had masterminded a robust economic recovery, eliminated the scourge of unemployment, re-established law and order, restored national pride and made Germany a force to be reckoned with in international affairs.

From this base of strength, Hitler embarked on an imperial drive, starting World War II and invading and conquering most of Europe and parts of Russia. In the process, Germany systematically eliminated 6MM Jewish and Slavic peoples and caused the deaths of over 25MM people in Europe and Russia, including five million of its own people. But, Germany was left in ruins. It took Germany a decade, after its unconditional surrender to the Allied forces, to recover from the destruction that took place during the war. The short-lived return to greatness was not worth the costs.

Imperial Japan: Beginning in the 17th century, Japan isolated itself from the modern world for over two hundred and fifty years. That isolation ended in 1853, with the arrival of four United States warships commanded by Commodore Matthew Perry. Perry sailed into Tokyo Bay and, using gunboat diplomacy, forced the Japanese to open the country up to U.S. trade and other exchanges. Lacking up-to-date military capabilities, the Japanese had little choice but to accede to the wishes of this powerful adversary and eventually bow to similar demands from European nations as well.

Over the ensuing decades, the Japanese had to swallow a great deal of pride. They were compelled to accept unequal status relative to European Powers in all treaties with the West. They were forced to give back territory won in the first Sino-Japanese war in 1904 and to endure the embarrassment of being subjected to severe restrictions on Japanese immigration into the United States. These actions, taken by the West, were a grievous affront to the Japanese, all the more so because they viewed themselves as elite among nations, racially superior, and chosen by the Gods.

The shame that resulted provided the fuel for a massive transformation. Beginning with the Meiji Restoration in 1867, the Japanese leaders recognized that they had to make sweeping changes if they were ever going to be able to resist the demands of other countries, establish themselves as an equal of the great Western powers, and end the disgrace they felt from being obliged to accept an inferior position in global affairs. They realized that they were going to have to rapidly modernize their economy, dramatically improve their military capabilities, and reorganize their system of governance so as create a structure and practices more consistent with those of a modern European state. Over the next two to three decades, they achieved all these goals.

The outcome was a stunning turnaround in Japanese power and influence. Japan won a series of small-scale wars at the turn of the century--the Sino-Japanese War in 1894, the Russo-Japanese War in 1904, and the Korean-Japanese War in 1905. Then it annexed Korea in 1910, invaded Manchuria in 1931 and China in 1937. In the early 1940's, Japan attacked the United States in the Pacific, conquered most of Southeast Asia, including the Philippines, Indonesia, Indo-China, and a string of Pacific Islands. By late 1942, Japan's national revival seemed to be a staggering success.

But, it came at great cost to others, and ultimately to the Japanese themselves, as they were forced to accept the ultimate humiliation of an unconditional surrender. Japan's imperial wars led to the deaths of at least twenty to twenty-five million Chinese, Korean, Filipino, Indo-Chinese, Australian and American civilians and military personnel, and to the deaths of at close to four million Japanese. The return to greatness had failed.

Khmer Rouge Cambodia: In Cambodia, in the 1970's, a different brand of communist ideology materialized, one that reflected the both the principles of communism and the notion of returning the country to a golden age in the past. For the Khmer Rouge, the war in Indochina was their opportunity to seize control of society, impose their ideology, and create their own version of utopia. They harkened back to the ancient past--when the area that was now Cambodia was an empire in its own right--Angkor. They emphasized the greatness of Angkor, which is even now seen as one of the wonders of the ancient world.

To the Khmer Rouge, the appeal of Angkor was that it was created by the Cambodian nation, not by imperialist or colonialist powers, and that there were still visible symbols of that greatness in the ruins at Angkor Wat. They believed they could return their territory to its former Golden Age and their people to "a pristine rural condition," severing all interaction with the outside world and creating an agricultural revolution within the country.

To achieve this miracle, the people would have to rid themselves of their oppressors and drive out/kill all foreign, religious, and alien racial groups and regain former territory, which they claimed had been illegally taken by Vietnam. In addition, they created a vast network of slave labor, using anyone suspected of being an enemy of the state, to build dykes, levees, and dams to harness the water needed to expand significantly the level of agricultural production within the country. The plan was to gain needed foreign exchange and capital by growing and exporting vast amounts of rice.

To accomplish their objectives, they broke up families, worked people to death, turned children into soldiers, and killed anyone who objected or protested. The whole structure was held together through fear and violence, but collapsed when Vietnam invaded the country. Although the goal was a utopia of race, class, and nation, what was created was a hell on earth in which millions were slaughtered to achieve a complete transformation of society.

These four historical examples present a scary, but realistic, picture of the consequences of buying into the overused "Make a Nation Great Again" concept. Regardless of how it is approached, it is merely a tactic for leaders to get into and stay in power and nothing else. It never achieves its stated goal of creating a utopian society. It merely rationalizes many dangerous actions and programs that lead to misery for everyone. In spite of this reality, this concept never seems to die as an idea, no matter how the catastrophic the results. When it becomes the centerpiece of any political program that drives the future of a country, people should watch out and treat it with great skepticism and fear. It will end badly.

The second of the three dangerous ideas currently being pushed in America is truly frightening. Some people believe it would be acceptable if America shed its democratic ideals and governing structure and became an authoritarian dictatorship. This view is shocking because America has a rich history that is filled with people who have wanted and valued living in a democracy, which literally means "rule of the people." They endorsed a democracy because they wanted to choose elected officials by free and secret ballot. They did not want their lives controlled by any one person or group. They needed to be able to express their individuality within a society operating under the principles of the rule of law.

But now, when people in the United States, especially evangelical Christians and people on the ideological right, are asked how they feel about America becoming an absolute dictatorship, they appear to be fine with it.[1] The current Republican Presidential candidate, reflecting his stated admiration for dictators around the world, has aggressively exploited this trend. He has outlined in some detail, how he will seek to move the country to an authoritarian form of government if he is elected President in the 2024 election.

The problem is that many of those Americans who favor authoritarianism have never lived in a dictatorship. As a result, they have no sense of how bad life would be if it, in fact, happened. What they don't realize is that when people allow absolutist ideas to creep into society, they are opening the door to very deadly consequences, which they will hate when they experience them. Some examples of what has happened in the past when absolute governments take over a society are spelled out below.

Absolutist regimes kill people, often on a massive scale. They are much more likely than democratically constituted regimes to engage in mass murder, both of their own citizens and those of other countries. In a study analyzing dozens of mass killing incidents throughout human history, R.J. Rummel explained why some nations or groups commit mass murder and others don't. He specifically focused on the differences between open, democratic societies and closed, totalitarian societies to explain why the latter group has been more inclined to engage in this murderous behavior.

Rummel stated his initial hypothesis, which was subsequently validated by his extensive research, that more democratic nations are less likely to commit foreign or domestic mass murder. His theory is that normal democratic processes and the pluralism of free societies will impose restraints on decision makers and power centers and focus everyone on rational debate, negotiation, and tolerance of different views. These forces would help avoid the conflict and violence that occurs in more absolutist societies. On the opposite side of the fence are totalitarian political regimes:

> "...Rather than being a means for resolving differences in views, they try to impose, upon society, a particular ideology, religion, or solution to social problems, regardless of the opposition. For this

reason, such regimes try to control all aspects of society and deal with conflict by force and fear, that is, by power. Moreover, such power breeds political paranoia by the dictator or a narrow ruling group. The fear is that others are always plotting to take over rule and would execute those now in power. Democide becomes a device to rule, as in eliminating possible opponents, or a means for achieving one's ideological goal, as in the purification of one's country of an alien race or the reconstruction of society."[2]

My own research into mass killing has also confirmed the idea that the most prolific mass murderers occurred under the most absolute dictatorships. Communist governments easily killed over one hundred million people. Three of history's most deadly autocratic regimes, Imperial China, Imperial Japan, and Nazi Germany were responsible for the deaths of close to one hundred million people in their efforts to conquer other countries and eliminate hated others. Christian and Islamist theocracies, run as religious dictatorships, slaughtered tens of millions to ensure their dominance over all other sects and faiths. And many autocratic, pre-modern societies were aggressive and brutal conquerors and killers of other peoples. Tamerlane and his followers, the Mongols, and the Manchu are thought to have killed at least twenty million each as they carried out their aggressive territorial conquests during the thirteenth through sixteenth centuries.

But mass killing is not the only deadly outcome that has emerged from the acceptance of absolute ideologies. Leadership groups that have adopted absolutist approaches to thinking and governing, even if they don't massacre millions, usually default, over time, to more and more extreme methods to govern society and sustain their political domination of their country. As Rummel noted above, absolute dictators do fear opposition and become increasingly paranoid about possible enemies who might seek to overthrow them. It is rumored, for example, that Vladimir Putin of Russia repeatedly watched the film of the deaths of Saddam Hussein and Muammar Gaddafi as a constant reminder of the threat that disloyal people represent to his regime.

As a result, over the two dozen years that Putin has been President of Russia, he has moved aggressively to protect himself from being overthrown by his elites and his own people. To accomplish this goal, his regime has become increasingly repressive, violent, and isolated. Opponents are violently and often cruelly repressed; enemies are tortured

PATH TO POWER, ROAD TO RUIN

or assassinated; dissent is severely punished; the judicial system becomes a tool of the security services; ideological propaganda is amped up to extreme levels; and no one is allowed to challenge Putin in any way.

As a result, he has made himself "President for Life." Now, he can operate with impunity, stealing the assets of the state for his own benefit, taking down successful companies to make sure no one has as much power as he does, starting illegitimate wars which he conducts brutally without censure, killing and imprisoning his opponents without proper due process, and building an extensive state security operation.

The recent death of Alexei Navalny marks a watershed in his twenty-five year drive to rid himself of all opponents. While in the early years of his reign, there were street protests, an opportunity for self-expression on the part of ordinary citizens, elections of a sort, some independent media, and foreign NGO's operating in Russia, now there is nothing. With Navalny's demise, Putin no longer has any opposition. He is a totalitarian dictator and will remain in total control for the indefinite future, while his society decays around him.

The same types of things are happening in other countries governed by absolutist regimes, including, but not limited to China, North Korea, and Iran. The leaders of these countries, Xi Jinping, Kim Jong Un, and Ali Khamenei, share Putin's approach to governing. They have forgone normal due process and installed themselves as permanent rulers. They kill, imprison, or eliminate anyone who opposes them, anyone who they suspect is disloyal, and anyone who acquires too much power in any sector of society—even attacking successful businessmen and breaking up their companies. They have absolutely no compunction about using extreme violence against protesters, killing people, ruining their lives, and taking what they want when it serves their special interest. Their aim is to create fear that kills all impulse to protest or rebel.

When countries move down the path to dictatorship, it can take a long time for them to return to the way they were, if they do at all. Absolute governments are remarkably sticky, lasting for decades and even centuries, making life miserable for the people who live under their regimes. Autocratic regimes generally only disappear under one of two circumstances, i.e., when they are conquered by outsiders—much as Japan and Germany were in World War II--or when they rot and collapse from within—as the Ottoman Empire did in the late nineteenth and early twentieth centuries and the Soviet Union did in the late twentieth century.

People who live in an autocratic system have to live in extreme fear, as anyone can be punished severely without warning and without due process, whether they are guilty or not. Laws, to the extent that they exist, are typically vaguely worded so they can be applied in any way and at any time, even after the fact. For example, in the Soviet era, people were rounded up and arrested without warrant, just because they belonged to a targeted group or their arrest was required to make a quota.

Once they were in custody, their guilt and prosecution was inevitable. Nothing the accused said or did could exculpate them. Their investigators beat and tortured them to gain confessions of wrong doing or ideological deviance. As part of that confession, they were forced to give the names of other people whom the investigators should arrest. And those people were then put through the same process as well.

Any individual could give anyone's name without any proof of wrong doing. Once identified, victims were railroaded through the process, destined for execution. They had no recourse whatsoever. Whatever the prosecutor decided prevailed, as those arrested were found guilty 95+% of the time. The testimony of witnesses was not seriously considered. The defense was severely restrained from presenting a proper case. So, once the accused were in the system, their fate was decided.

People who live in autocratic states have no control of their lives. Everything, even personal morality, is dictated by the state. In China today, the government has created a behavioral model that specifies what is considered acceptable behavior in society. It tracks everyone on cameras which are recording everything that is happening everywhere. It matches every person in society with facial recognition software, allowing the authorities to keep a record of every individual's behavior. It rewards and punishes everyone based on their observed conduct and also that of their friends and relatives. The punishments take away, among other things, people's right to travel or enjoy certain basic societal privileges. Unfortunately, the use of technology to exercise totalitarian domination over society is only going to increase. Dictators will soon be able see everything and exercise complete control over all things that people say, do, and ultimately even think.

In an authoritarian regime, the arbitrary application of justice is the rule, not the exception. People in power can target anyone and demand whatever they want of that person because they have the ability to make people any pay dearly for a lack of compliance. If an important or powerful official wants a woman to sleep with him, he merely threatens to have her or her loved ones put in jail or shot. If he needs someone to commit a crime for him, he will; and his agent will be forced to comply or face serious consequences. If he gets caught, only he will suffer. If an employer decides not to pay his employees for their hard work, they have no recourse. When the local governments in China, for example, decided to expropriate an individual's land, there was generally nothing the victim could do to stop it.[3]

When citizens get imprisoned in dictatorships, they really suffer. As Aleksandr Solzhenitsyn warned us in his book, *The Gulag Archipelago*, one of the worst things about being a political prisoner was that the incarcerated had to mix with a violent criminal population when they were in prison and when they were being transported to prison.[4] They were punished triply—they were imprisoned for long periods of time, mixed with hardened violent criminals who beat and exploited them; and turned into slave laborers that had to work long hours under brutal conditions with inadequate food and limited sleep. They had absolutely no regulatory or other protections to save them or mitigate their condition.

The point is that, as ordinary citizens, people who live in absolutist environments are powerless. Their fate is decided by others. How they live and think is determined by others. They are constantly exposed to the arbitrary actions of authorities who control everyone's lives. Individuals have no say; their future is strictly limited.

Even their opportunity for personal wealth creation is subject to the whims of the leaders' choice about how to manage the economy and allocate resources. Disproportionate amounts of money are allocated to defense and internal security, which drains the resources of the main economy. Or, money is siphoned off from the system by corrupt officials stealing the resources of the state. Or, flawed state planning processes, guided by subjective decision-making lead to bad economic choices. As a result, the economy underperforms its potential and ordinary people, not the leaders or the elites, suffer the consequences.

And there is no escape. Even those who think they are part of a favored group and therefore will be safe, can suddenly be targeted for elimination. Some of the most loyal cadres with the finest revolutionary credentials have been eliminated in every communist country. The fact that they were champions of the regime or enthusiastically embraced the required belief system did not save them. The reason: paranoid autocratic rulers have great fear of anyone they cannot control or who builds an independent power base, even within their own regime. We know that many of the most powerful men in Russia and China have been removed from their positions and killed or imprisoned in the last few years. No one is safe in an absolutist government.

No matter how frustrated you are with your life, no matter how badly off you think you are in a democratic society, no matter how poorly you think your interests are being served, you do not want to live in a dictatorship. You will be much worse off, because you will have no opportunity to change society and you have a much higher chance of being brutalized on an almost unimaginable scale without any due process. Living in a democracy is a rare gift. We must not put it at risk. Dictatorship is not a solution to our country's issues.

The third of the three dangerous ideas is that it is perfectly acceptable for a country to exclude or marginalize certain groups and restrict their rights and access to the benefits of our society.

As I mentioned in the supremacy chapter of this book, people's relative position in this world is very important to them; and they will go to great lengths to reinforce their claim that they are superior and others are inferior. For example, we know that there are people on the ideological right who want to turn this country into a white male Christian society. They would relegate women to roles in the home, depriving them of the right to pursue careers or make decisions about their own bodies. They would deport one million illegal immigrants, marginalize minorities and people of color, and prevent certain groups from voting.

They continue to take this stand even though human history has shown that the validity of the many supremacist claims made by religious, political, economic, and social groups in the United States and globally, do not stand up to serious scrutiny. The presumption that any one group of humans is *sustainably* superior or inferior to any other group is simply erroneous. While, it is true that certain groups or individuals can build temporary advantages that may last for a while, most do not. Eventually, their advantage dissipates as new competitors emerge on the scene and rise to their full potential.

The ascendancy of all groups is cyclical, not permanent. A group may appear superior for a while and seem invincible, but they will soon give up their position of dominance. For example, when a particular societal group, like the Mongols, entered a region with new weapons or war-making skills, they were able to rise rapidly to the top. The Mongols brought superb horsemanship and new tactics to the battle space when they invaded westward across Asia into the Middle East and Europe. They easily defeated everyone they encountered and killed thirty million or more people, sowing terror and fear everywhere they went. But, even their hold on the countries they conquered ultimately dissipated.

The Mongols were not alone. Throughout history, every single empire that has accumulated great power and wealth has inevitably fallen. Egypt, Mesopotamia, Persia, Assyria, Greece, Rome, the Vandals, the Goths, the Ottoman Empire, the Aztecs and Incas in Central America, Great Britain, Nazi Germany, Imperial Japan, and Russia all once had substantial empires that were subsequently lost to the next conqueror or the ravages of time. Not one could sustain its position of dominance.

Also, there is a flip side to this issue. People that are on the bottom of the hierarchical scale and that have been suppressed for decades or centuries, like the Irish under British rule, the Blacks in the American South, the lower castes in India, or people in third world countries have often been characterized as losers, lazy, stupid, apelike. However, once they free themselves from the bonds of oppression, they often rise to high levels of performance and become quite successful. Regardless of their race, ethnicity, nationality, gender and religion, all groups or individuals are capable of achieving great things once they are given the opportunity to do so.

For example, after being dominated for decades, even centuries, many of the colonies of the great European imperial empires overcame significant economic, technological, and cultural disadvantages and subsequently rose to great heights. They were once thought of as backward and barbarian cultures, almost savages, that could easily be manipulated and controlled by the West. They were viewed as incapable of self-government or efficient development of their own resources. Since then, these former colonies, like China, India, South Korea, and Indonesia have all become major players on the world stage. They have achieved significant economic growth, seized leadership of major industries, developed breakthrough technologies, and, in many ways, easily surpassed their Western European exploiters.

Women have been and still are being told that they belong in the home and patted on the head when they say that they want something more, i.e., to pursue careers and other objectives, beyond child-rearing and homemaking. Their capabilities are disparaged; and their achievements belittled. They are called "cat ladies." Yet today, as women have begun to break the bonds of traditional roles, they are proving themselves to be the equal of men. They are more likely to complete their college degrees than men. They are getting more advanced degrees and more PHD's than men. They are becoming doctors, lawyers, professors, business executives, and holding public office in greater numbers. They are accomplishing much, but many men still try to keep them down.

It is clear, from an historical perspective, that the idea that certain people or groups are sustainably superior or inferior to others, does not stand up to close scrutiny. Further, scientific and DNA analyses also demonstrate that no particular group has any inherent genetic advantages over any other. Genetic research has demonstrated that the differences between nations, races, classes, are no greater than the differences among individuals within each of these groups. Kwame Anthony, an NYU Professor, in an article in *Foreign Affairs,* makes three points that further strengthen this argument.

> "The differences found between the geographic populations of the human species were differences in gene frequencies rather than differences in some putative racial essence..."

> "National, religious, geographic, linguistic, and cultural groups do not necessarily coincide with racial traits; and the cultural traits of such groups have not demonstrated genetic connections with racial traits..."

> "The scientific material available to us at present does not justify the conclusion that inherited genetic differences are a major factor in producing differences between the cultures and cultural achievements of different peoples or groups."[5]

In other words, the idea that one particular race or group of people is inherently superior to any another group, and thus deserves special treatment, really has no scientific or historical validity. They are all human social constructions and flawed and serve only to limit the achievements of our society. If we are going to maximize the potential of everyone in our society, we must adopt a more inclusive stance.

This is of critical importance today because the United States is now facing the most dangerous and effective competitor that it has ever faced in its history as a nation, i.e., Communist China. China has the largest economy in the world on a purchasing power parity basis. It has

          PATH TO POWER, ROAD TO RUIN

a substantial positive trade balance with the US and most countries in
the world, and, as a result, has significant foreign exchange reserves to
fall back on in a crisis. Many of its companies are global leaders in their
industries; and it has leading edge technologies in areas that are crucial
for future development.

China has one billion four hundred million people, four times
our three hundred and fifty million. More people, especially more
educated people, means that the Chinese have more labor to support their
economy, their scientific research and development, their innovation,
their new products, and all the things that can give them an economic
and military edge over us. And they are dedicating enormous resources to
building up their military to be on a par with the United States.

If we are going to compete in this environment, we need to have
all our people working up to their full capability. We can't force women
into the home to have babies if they want to pursue scientific or senior
level positions that can advance our country's position vs. our competitive
set. We can't deport all immigrants or remove foreigners from the country
if we want to have the labor resources to keep our economy growing
and be able to provide the cash flow needed to invest in research and
development for our citizens' well-being. We cannot afford to tolerate
the supremacist and exclusivist attitudes held by the more conservative
members of our society. We must be an inclusive society to have real
competitive strength.

The three dangerous ideas discussed in this chapter are
increasingly dominating the American and even the world political
scene. Americans believe they are immune to the forces, which lead to
dictatorship, but they are not. These seductive ideological themes that
keep arising around the world have recurred again and again throughout
history, even though they lack validity and need to be rejected. Instead
of indulging in these bad ideas, we need to ask ourselves: Is there a better
way? Is there a road to a better future?

Chapter 8

THE ROAD TO A BETTER FUTURE

Ideologies have always been problematic. They have consistently had serious consequences for humanity; the claims and promises they make to justify their acceptance have proven to be false and misleading; they have always disguised their true purpose; and they have consistently been used to manipulate and control people and make them submissive to those in power. Given these stark realities, we should, in the interests of humanity, consider rejecting, or at least significantly modifying, the acceptance and use of these types of belief systems.

The problem we have is that once people embrace ideologies, it can be extraordinarily challenging to motivate them to break free of their entrenched belief systems or to conduct an objective assessment of their beliefs. People's acceptance of religious and political ideologies is ultimately motivated and sustained by how well these ideologies relieve their anxieties, assuage their doubts and fears, satisfy their desires, address their needs, and provide them with the certainties they require to survive in this life. When people accept and embrace ideologies for these types of reasons, they inevitably have little interest in disputing their validity. They are just too emotionally vested in their beliefs to break away.

Further, neuroscience has demonstrated that once people's beliefs are formed, it is very difficult to modify or eliminate them. Greg Lester, in his article, *Why Bad Beliefs Won't Die*, explains why:

> "The brain is a stubborn organ. Once its primary set of beliefs has been established, the brain finds it difficult to integrate opposing ideas and beliefs. This…helps to explain why some people cannot abandon destructive beliefs, be they religious, political or psychological…"In fact, the survival value of the beliefs is based on their ability to persist in the face of contradictory evidence. The brain doesn't care whether belief matches the data. It cares

whether the belief is helpful to survival. That is why beliefs—
even bad, irrational, or crazy beliefs don't die in the face of
contradictory evidence."[1]

While there is little doubt that the transition away from
ideological forms of thinking will be difficult, there is no reason to
give up on the important goal of reducing the impact of these more
consequential belief systems. The required change needs to happen.

The easiest thing to do would be to wait for belief system flaws
and failures to shrink ideologies' base of committed followers to the point
where they are no longer so influential. History has shown that ideologies
can weaken and even disappear in the face of real-world pressures:

First, when an ideology fails to sustain an economically and
socially viable political system in the real world, people will, if given
the choice, discard the belief system as unworkable. For example,
communism, in all its many variants, became discredited when virtually
all communist countries proved unable to compete effectively against
their most important ideological competitors, i.e., democratic, capitalist
societies. The Soviet Union could not keep up with the United States
economically, technologically, or militarily. Western European countries
easily surpassed their communist counterparts in Eastern European.
And South Korea's economy grew rapidly while North Korea stagnated.
Capitalism won every one of these head-to-head competitions and
exposed communism's fundamental weaknesses.

The theories proposed by Marx, Engels, Lenin, and others were
just not viable in the real world. Eventually, their flaws and vulnerabilities
resulted in each of the communist systems, either becoming sclerotic and
collapsing internally, as was the case for the Soviet Union and Eastern
Europe, degrading into corrupt totalitarian dictatorships, as has been
the case in North Korea and Cuba, or emerging in a completely different
form, as is the case in China, where communism, as defined by Marx and
Engels no longer really exists. The only thing that has been retained are
the Marxist/Leninist governance and social systems.

Second, when belief systems commit horrific crimes, people
may eventually be highly motivated to reject them in their entirety.
National Socialism disappeared as a mainstream ideology in 1945, after
the military defeat of its leading proponent, Nazi Germany. However,
its more dangerous elements, i.e., the extreme nationalism and racism it
espoused, continue to reappear as potent and destructive ideologies in

                    PATH TO POWER, ROAD TO RUIN

their own right.

Finally, when ideologies, in particular religious belief systems, have not lived up to the ideals they require of their followers or have failed to keep up with the times, they can gradually lose credibility and see a reduction in follower participation and commitment. Consumer surveys about religion in America, conducted by Pew Research, have demonstrated that there has recently been a marked increase in those who say they have no religion or are religiously unaffiliated--26% of respondents in 2019, up from 17% in 2007. Further, the youngest age groups are leading this change and are almost four times as likely as oldest age groups to be unaffiliated—40% percent of millennials claim they are unaffiliated vs 11% of the silent generation.

Additionally, there are now many more survey respondents who say they never attend religious services. In the early 1970's, 11% said they never attend. Now, it's 27%. Also, there has been a marked decrease in those who identify as Christian, 65% of respondents in 2019, down from 77% in 2007. Additionally, the situation in Europe and Latin America is even more dramatic. They now have lowest church attendance in the entire world. And finally, in North America, Europe, and Australia, a majority of people say religion should play less of role in society than it has in the past.[2]

There is clearly a basis for ideologies losing credibility with followers and, in a few cases, failing completely. But, while different belief systems may fail at a particular time and place, this does not mean that they cannot metamorphose and reoccur in another time and place. For example, the idea of returning a country to its former greatness, mentioned earlier in this book, keeps being the "go-to" ideology for many countries where the people believe that they have experienced a significant decline in status.

These recurrences reflect the reality that belief systems' strong link with human needs and fears means that people will continue to buy into their failed premises, whenever they haven't personally experienced a disastrous outcome from the implementation of the ideology or they haven't studied enough history to be aware of the consequences that have occurred in the past. Therefore, it is not likely that belief systems will easily die out on their own, at least not in the short-term. Instead, they will have to be pushed out of the limelight forcefully.

This is the main reason why I felt compelled to write this book, i.e., to make people aware of the high cost of buying into ideological beliefs and the complete lack of validity of the claims they make. Given this information, the hope is that motivated individuals will make the effort to follow one of the several recommendations for change that are made in ensuing pages of this chapter.

The first thing that might make it easier for people to walk away from their existing, more dangerous ideologies would be if they could retain the benefits of having a structured belief system without having to accept the ideas that generate the worst consequences for humanity. The premise is that, if ideologies can't be made to disappear through gradual persuasion and education, then perhaps they can be modified to excise or minimize their most dangerous components. People might succeed in making ideologies less consequential by deconstructing them and extracting their most harmful elements, specifically removing:

1. The utopian thinking that causes people to believe they can create the perfect world by forcibly transforming mankind, often using brutal violence and pursuing their goals without any regard for the consequences of their actions;
2. The supremacist attitudes that lead people to disrespect, dehumanize or demonize hated or feared others, as a prelude to dominating, exploiting, or even eliminating them from their societies;
3. The absolutist views that shut out rational consideration and acceptance of alternative ways of thinking and favor the exercise of totalitarian control over everything people do, say, and even think.

A safer set of elements, on the other hand, would include ideas that are the exact antithesis of these three beliefs:

1. Embracing realistic, non-utopian, views that guide people to recognize that this world is all there is, that the human condition is extremely difficult, that this life does not lend itself to ideal or utopian outcomes; and that better lives come from everyone working hard on making the world a better place;
2. Adopting thinking that views all other inhabitants of the planet as equal and deserving of respect, regardless of their position in life or their class, nation, race, ethnicity, gender;
3. Encouraging people to grow intellectually by espousing flexible, non-dogmatic thinking and encouraging people to seek new perspectives, expand their knowledge, and develop an improved

                                        PATH TO POWER, ROAD TO RUIN

understanding of life, rather than treating beliefs as absolute ideas that cannot be questioned or modified.

Fortunately, there are two widely-followed, existing belief systems, Buddhism and Humanism, that actively embrace "safer" ideology components while eliminating their more dangerous counterparts. It is interesting that these two systems provide the benefits of the more controversial belief systems, without their bad outcomes, their serious validity issues, and their dependence on supernatural thinking.

The first alternative belief system involves embracing the *philosophical* tenets of Buddhism. I stress the philosophy rather than the Buddhist religion, because the established religion has historically violated its own principles in the past—when Myanmar's Buddhists contributed to the slaughter of Muslims in their country and when Tibetan Buddhists presided over an exploitive feudal order before the Chinese conquest in the 1950's.

One possible proposal would be to focus solely on the Buddha's original philosophical teachings, before his followers turned them into a formalized religion, created multiple sects and many different doctrines, and then began to incur all the problems that are attached to institutionalized religions today. A brief summary of the Buddha's teaching follows. It can be supplemented by reading the very approachable book, *The Beginner's Guide to Walking the Buddha's Eightfold Path.*[3]

The first part of the teaching is called the Fourfold Noble Truths. They can be very briefly summarized as follows: That this life is suffering; that suffering is the direct result of human craving and attachment to the impermanent things of this world; that it is possible to end this suffering by eliminating our clinging to transitory things, like fame, fortune, power, and sensual desires; and that there is a series of steps, known as the Eightfold Noble Path, that one can take to achieve a better life. Each of the eight steps is described below:

Right View is the ability to fully grasp the Fourfold Noble Truths, to gain insight into the realities of this life, to understand why we suffer, and to learn what we need to do end that suffering;

Right Intention is the recognition that, to end our suffering, we must dedicate ourselves to a life of ethical and mental self-improvement, focusing on learning to neutralize the pull of desire and the destructive influence of anger, while ensuring we do no harm to others;

Right Speech is the ethical commitment never to tell lies, slander others, speak in harsh and abusive language, or engage in idle gossip;

Right Action means to abstain from taking the life of any living being, from taking what is not willingly given, from engaging in sexual misconduct, or from abusing alcohol and drugs. It is based on the principle that wholesome actions produce positive outcomes while unwholesome actions lead to the opposite;

Right Livelihood says that to earn one's living in a righteous way, wealth should be gained legally and peacefully. People should avoid businesses that exploit or harm others or that trade in weapons, drugs, and intoxicants;

Right Effort is a prerequisite for achieving progress on the path of enlightenment. We have to be prepared to expend significant mental and physical energy and effort to accomplish meaningful change. And we have to be prepared to do it for years. Our goal is to restrain and abandon unwholesome mental states and to preserve wholesome mental states;

Right Mindfulness requires us to live in the present, to see things as they are right now, and employ disciplined thought processes in pursuit of enlightenment. The four foundations of mindfulness are the contemplation of the body, the mind, feelings, and phenomena;

Right Concentration occurs where all mental faculties are unified onto one particular object, concentrating on wholesome thoughts and actions, through the practice of meditation.

These actions represent focused solutions, designed to address life's difficulties and offer suggestions about what the individual can do to resolve them. They teach skills for personal development and control instead of turning life decisions over to others or to a particular ideology. They succeed by building the personal strength and resilience to cope with life issues and anxieties. They establish clear ethical standards to guide their followers' lives and make them more moral, considerate, and respectful human beings. Additionally, they provide simple add-on techniques, like meditation and Dialectic Behavioral Therapy, that build on Buddhist philosophical principles and help people reduce their anxiety, emotional pain, and suffering.

In addition to Buddhism, there is a second alternative belief system, e.g., Secular Humanism, that systematically rejects ideological solutions to life problems and specifically avoids the most dangerous components of the leading religious and political belief systems. While these ideas are controversial for many conservative religionists, they establish some very useful principles for living a good life. Humanism, in its more secular forms, consists of five core principles that effectively eliminate the need to indulge in utopian, supremacist, and absolutist thinking.

> "It establishes a comprehensive life stance, touching every aspect of life, including issues of values, meaning and identity, and calls for grounding one's worldview at a universal level, using the methods demonstrated by science."

> "It holds that nature is all there is. People do not need to resort to mythical or supernatural explanations for human existence. Reliable knowledge is best obtained by querying nature using the scientific method."

> "It endorses emancipating the individual from the traditional controls by family, church, and state and empowering each person to set the terms of his or her own life."

> "It holds that ethics are consequential, to be judged by results. This is in contrast to so-called command ethics, in which right and wrong are defined in advance and attributed to divine or earthly authority."

> "It takes the view that ideology—whether religious or political— must be thoroughly and skeptically examined by each individual, subjected to peer review, and not simply accepted or rejected on faith."[4]

In addition to these core principles, Secular Humanism teaches that people should include all human beings in their circle of acceptance, treat everyone with dignity and respect, and that adopt a position of harmlessness, which means not to think or act cruelly, violently, or aggressively towards anyone; further, it transcends divisive loyalties to race, nationality, ethnicity, and gender, and seeks to secure fairness and justice for all humans. It relies on the application of reason and science to advance our understanding of the universe; it asks us to be open to new ideas and the advancement of knowledge in the place of clinging to ideological perspectives that require acceptance of myth, magic, and rejection of natural law; and it endorses the idea that happiness and redemption come from a continuous commitment to achieving significant self-improvement through discipline and hard work on oneself.

These are the core tenets behind humanist philosophy. As with Buddhist philosophy, they require that followers understand their basic principles, not only from the perspective of learning the underlying philosophy, but also in terms of mastering the practice of those principles in their daily lives. This integration of philosophy and practice helps ensure that the ideas and beliefs are lived throughout their daily lives.

Both these belief systems offer an all-inclusive philosophical stance that shows people how to address life's challenges and difficulties in a way that lessens existential anxiety, offers hope for a better life, reduces the causes of intergroup and interpersonal conflict, and gives certainty, structure, and meaning to life.

Both adopt a realistic view of this world and tailor their belief system to that view, without ever resorting to mythical or magical explanations or to the beliefs that have been proven to lead to disastrous outcomes for humanity.

Both demonstrate respect for all life, believe in humanity's potential, reject violence as a solution to mankind's problems, and are deeply committed to humanity's moral development and education.

Both recognize that building a belief system is a life's work requiring an open, inquisitive, and flexible mind, that is willing to conduct an unending search for the truth, using disciplined critical thinking and analysis techniques.

Adopting these more benevolent belief systems, in the place of traditional religious or political ideologies, provides an excellent way to break the power of mankind's attachment to the more dangerous and consequential ideas that have traditionally driven human belief systems.

But there is yet another important option for us to consider, beyond embracing existing belief systems. Instead of embracing beliefs created by others, we could decide to develop our own beliefs. We could alter our method of formulating, vetting, and accepting beliefs, shedding the ideological approach used by most people in favor of adopting the superior analytical methodology used by a select group of very successful individuals. A comparison of these two approaches follows.

An ideological approach has certain well-defined characteristics that highlight its limitations as a belief formation tool. Ideologies are typically constructed using top-down processes. They are presented as fixed packages of beliefs, constructed by leaders and aggressively disseminated to their followers, as is, without discussion or debate.

Ideologies address powerful human needs, including the elimination of doubt and uncertainty, the reduction of existential anxiety, and the support of human ego and belonging requirements. As a result, they are typically constructed from ideas that we want to be true or need to be true, not what has been proven to be true.

Ideologies are built from unreliable sources, such as supposed revelations from God and his prophets, quotes from "sacred" texts, personal testimony, faith, feelings, and hopes. These are all things that cannot be verified or falsified, which means that ideological positions have to be accepted without proper foundation, and therefore, have to be considered untrustworthy.

Ideologies are principles-based, not consequences-based. When people create or endorse beliefs in this manner, they start by subjectively asserting a set of principles that become the basis for all their thought. They are not concerned with the outcomes or consequences of implementing these principles. They merely accept them as prima-facie-true. This makes them very dangerous. No idea should be accepted without understanding the outcomes that will flow from its acceptance and implementation.

Ideological thinking is inherently inflexible. Once established, it is almost impossible to effect changes in people's beliefs or to modify their ideologically-based positions. The problem is, that if an ideologue concedes that it is acceptable to doubt or reject some of his beliefs, then he would be effectively undermining his own authoritativeness and credibility with followers. It would be tantamount to admitting that his ideology and his core beliefs could be ignored.

Finally, ideologists do not want people thinking for

themselves. They want followers to blindly accept their dictates and turn responsibility for their lives and their beliefs over to them. They consciously seek to retard followers' ability to reason for themselves. Many ideology leaders consider human reasoning to be the ultimate evil act. They often say "reason is the tool of the devil." To be successful, ideologues need their followers to be passive recipients of whatever they are told; and to follow and obey the ideologies' dictates to the letter of the law.

Analytical thinking, on the other hand, is the antithesis of an ideological approach and has distinctly different characteristics.

Analytic thinking proceeds from the ground up, not from the top down. It is developed by individuals or small groups working together on an issue by issue basis to come up with valid, fact-based beliefs.

Analytic approaches require a commitment to doing investigative work and fact gathering to make certain that all beliefs are grounded in real data. Ideas that are not rigorously tested in this way are rejected as just personal, faith-based positions which cannot be verified or falsified and, therefore, have little validity.

Analytical methods reject principles-first approaches, typical in ideological thinking, in favor of those that require an assessment of outcomes before accepting any belief. How an idea works out when implemented in the real world is fundamental to establishing its validity or invalidity. To embrace and support beliefs without understanding their impact and their ability to cause real human suffering is criminal.

Analytical thinking acknowledges the reality of life and tries to operate within that reality. It is therefore concerned with knowing the truth about life and building beliefs that are consistent with objective reality, not opinion, guesses, faith-based propositions, and other unsubstantiated claims.

Analytic thinking processes are specifically designed to be subject to continuous change and alteration as new and better information comes to the fore. They recognize that the truth advances as belief positions and processes get developed, modified, and improved over time. Valid beliefs incorporate new information and new knowledge as they arise. They adapt to a changing world instead of locking their ideas in place. Superior evidence-based belief systems adjust. Inferior ideological ones do not.

The importance of having accurate beliefs is most powerfully demonstrated by looking at the successes achieved by people who use fact-based analytical approaches to deal with life as opposed to those

                                    PATH TO POWER, ROAD TO RUIN

who use anecdotes, conspiracy theories, propaganda, and other subjective approaches to making decisions.

First, from the business world, in 2007/8, business leaders, such as the US Treasury Secretary, the Federal Reserve Chairman, finance and real estate executives, investment bankers, financial advisors, and rating agencies all asserted that residential mortgages would never default and that they were very attractive and safe investments. The reality turned out to be quite different. Billions of dollars of mortgages did, in fact, default, bringing down major financial institutions worldwide, driving the global economy to the verge of collapse, putting millions of people out of work, and causing the worst economic and financial crisis since the Great Depression.

Most people, who just blindly accepted the assurances of Wall Street and the rating agencies and didn't do their own independent thinking, suffered severe investment losses. On the other hand, a handful of smart, hard-working people, including Michael Burry of Scion Capital, Steven Eisman of Front Point Capital, and Jamie Mai, Charlie Ledley, and Ben Hockett of Cornwall Capital, all did their own extensive, in-depth research into the mortgage market, the quality of the securities offered, mortgage delinquency data, the validity of rating agency assessments, and then went into the field to see what was actually happening in the marketplace.

They unearthed a very different view of the market. They decided the whole business was on the verge of collapse, and proceeded to short mortgages securities as well as the stock of companies operating in the field. They took brutal criticism from their owners/investors for taking a position that contradicted conventional wisdom; and, in addition, every month that they retained their short position, they had to pay a substantial monthly premium to their securities originators. But, because they were so confident in their data, they were able to stick with their position and, in the end, they made staggering sums of money. The superior financial outcome was the direct result of their having undertaken research and analysis efforts that let them understand the objective reality of the business that almost everyone else, including the rating agencies and the bankers, completely missed.[5]

A second example comes from the world of sports. Building a baseball franchise and recruiting top players is a challenging enterprise. It historically was a business run by scouts, managers, and team owners based on subjective experience, individual perception, tradition, instincts, and myth.

Billy Beane, the General Manager of the Oakland A's changed the structure of the business by exploiting the significant statistical information available, but not effectively used, in baseball. He was really the first to take advantage of the available data to develop a set of quantitative success factors for the game. He debunked many baseball myths perpetrated by the group that historically made talent and game decisions based on gut instincts and subjective judgment. For example, the "old guard" believed in the value of bunting, stealing bases, and drafting high school vs. college players, while his data suggested they hurt rather than helped performance. Beane stressed instead the critical importance of runs scored, on-base percentages and walks. He used his analysis findings and conclusions to acquire a set of players that would fit the newly developed success factors, that allowed his team to the produce the league-leading offense with the second lowest player salary budget of any team in Major League Baseball. He did this, in spite of significant resistance from his scouts, his manager, and his coaches. The result: Oakland won more games with less money than any other team in the league, demonstrating the superiority of facts and evidence over tradition, outmoded practices, and subjective impressions. The benefit of Beane's fact-based approach was eroded away as other teams saw what Oakland was doing, copied them, and even advanced the science. But that doesn't negate the value of Beane's fact-based, analytic approach.[6]

A third illustration of the power of analytical thinking evolves from a study of wars between countries. In warfare, detailed information about the whereabouts of enemy troop concentrations, positions, movements, and available weaponry will inevitably be decisive. Those who have correct information about the reality of the battlespace, and actually put it to use, will have a stunning advantage over those who don't. Once again, having the facts and understanding objective reality will be decisive. In war, as in life, unsupported beliefs will fail.

During the Gulf War in 1990-91, this information advantage proved decisive. The side that was flying blind lost badly.

"The fight looked to be a tough one; but it wasn't... The reason: tactical information systems worked reliably, and the creation of the Joint Surveillance and Target Acquisition System, so closely interlinked to all friendly forces, worked at the broader operational level to give the Allies a full synoptic view of the battlespace. By comparison Saddam Hussein's troops had to fight virtually blind. It was this information edge that enabled a lopsided victory to be won in just over 96 hours of operations on the ground. To many, this desert victory signaled the possibility of a true revolution in military affairs – –one largely driven by advances in information technologies."[7]

The world's top investors, like Warren Buffet, Ray Dalio, and Howard Marks consistently outperform other investors, by gathering, reviewing, and analyzing as much insightful information as possible on potential investment opportunities. In the investment management business, success requires lots of research and a very good understanding about what was going on in industries and companies. Top investment performance requires good facts and analysis. Those with the best, most realistic, understanding of what's happening in the marketplace, will tend to have the best results over time. The same is true for individual company business and financial performance. Those companies that have a realistic and up-to-date understanding of markets, competitors, and opportunities will win the battle for market share and achieve superior financial performance. Winners in the investment or corporate fields do not believe what they want to believe or need to believe or worry about what others tell them to believe. Instead, they win with objective factual information, especially information that others may not have.

Surprisingly, the techniques that help investors, business executives, sports managers, and military leaders achieve great successes also apply to ordinary people in their lives. For example, American psychotherapist, Albert Ellis, revolutionized modern psychotherapy by making sure that "reason, science, and rationality would remain top priorities in the evolution of psychotherapeutic techniques." In 1957, he developed a new approach to help his patients, called Rational Emotive Behavior Therapy or REBT. It has become a standard in the field. REBT practitioners use critical thinking and scientific methods to resolve the challenges of daily life.

"REBT practitioners challenge their clients to look for evidence to support unsound and harmful irrational beliefs and to test the assumptions behind them." "When clients recognize their beliefs as irrational, REBT therapists encourage them to adopt flexible and non-dogmatic alternative views. For example, instead of clinging to the anxiety provoking idea they must absolutely not be rejected by anyone, clients are encouraged to question whether rejection is catastrophic. In addition to teaching clients to think critically, REBT practitioners advocate humanistic values that increase the probability of living a healthy and happy existence."[8]

These examples help demonstrate the value of gathering fact-based evidence and using disciplined processes to develop belief positions that are consistent with objective reality. There are clear benefits to using analytic thinking and intensive information gathering to win life's competitive battles and become a psychologically and emotionally balanced person. Those advantages stand in stark relief to the very negative consequences of ideologically-driven beliefs.

However, one of the most compelling arguments for this approach is the way in which dictators behave with regard to the truth. Their immediate reaction is to run from and suppress the truth. It is far too scary for them.

Why? Because dictators absolutely know the value of the truth, even more so than many of their democratic counterparts. They demonstrate their understanding of the power of the truth, every day, by doing everything they can to kill it. They take down all internet posts revealing the truth. They eliminate or imprison anyone who tries to provide the truth, who overrides their censorship of the truth, or who overcomes their attempt to provide their distorted view of reality. They get rid of all independent media, arrest journalists, and use the sole remaining media outlets to reinforce their message.

If the truth weren't so dangerous to them, they would leave it alone. They know their views and actions are wrong and what they are doing is wrong. And most of all, they don't want to be held accountable. They know that if alternate beliefs were allowed to exist, then their status as leaders and their whole constructed belief system would be at risk. Their narrative must hold their followers or they will defect or revolt. Lies and fantasy are the only things that keep them afloat. The people who most deny access to the truth know its value better than anybody.

But how do we stop the widespread acceptance of unverifiable and unfalsifiable beliefs that are so prevalent today? The answer is that the influence of ideology and other man-made belief systems will only cease to be when people decide to put an end to accepting these ideas and not before. If people are going to stop allowing themselves to be manipulated by leaders, politicians, clergy, media outlets, and talking heads, they will have to change their attitudes about the truth. They have to want to know the objective truth. They have to want to find, well-documented, factual evidence for their beliefs. They have to feel it's worth their effort. They have to be motivated to shed old habits and beliefs. The end goal must be that no one will ever accept beliefs or ideas that they haven't verified or falsified themselves.

For this to happen, people would start forming their own beliefs, gathering their own evidence to support their views, and truly understanding what is going on in the world around them. Going forward, people would believe because they had first subjected their most consequential beliefs to intense scrutiny, extensive reading, thorough analysis, and systematic evaluation. They would use disciplined critical thinking processes to develop more rigorous belief systems that avoid the negative outcomes and implausible claims associated with existing utopian, supremacist, or absolutist ideologies. They would be prepared to read and learn more about other points of view, different from their own. They would study and evaluate all the claims that they have historically embraced to determine whether they really had any validity.

It will take time for most people to complete their own self-directed data gathering and analyses. And during that time, their position will be constantly evolving and improving. But that is fine. To simplify the process, people can break the belief evaluation process into manageable chunks that they can handle. They would begin by separately examining, over time, each of the most critical elements of their existing political and religious beliefs. They would divide them into discrete parts, and challenge each component's authority and veracity by gathering extensive information (literature search, reading books/articles, engaging in conversations), both pro and con, to allow them to understand all sides of the argument they are evaluating. Participants would proceed by analyzing each religious or political claim, narrative, and supposition on which their beliefs are based before deciding if each is likely to be true. The goal of this research process would need to determine if there is concrete, factual evidence that supports their belief positions. If there isn't, then those beliefs should be discarded.

There would be six basic pre-conditions required to achieve the quality of critical thinking necessary to developing well-grounded, bottoms-up belief systems. People who choose to do this would have:

1. To feel free to choose what they believe and not be subject to domineering outside influences, not be influenced by fear, threats, and intimidation, and not feel that they need to succumb to

social pressure about what they can and cannot think;

2. To be indifferent as to the outcome of their efforts. They must have no pre-existing mental commitments, no underlying biases, and no need-based or wishful thinking which could interfere with their plans to develop fact-based, objective positions;

3. To be willing to have their minds changed. If there isn't a basic openness to revising beliefs as the result of evidence, there is little point in making the investment of time required;

4. To have high standards about what they accept as evidence, either from others or from themselves. Research would have to be exhaustive and sufficient to justify rejecting existing claims made or establishing new or revised positions;

5. To accept only conclusions that are both intellectually honest and replicable, meaning, the research results can be repeated when studied from a different angle by different people;

6. To employ a rigorous, disciplined process which comes to appropriate conclusions. It should be evidence and fact-based, and focused on objective truth, not personal or philosophical truth as its ultimate goal. An effective process ideally would include the following steps:

    a. develop the questions that the belief research needs to address,

    b. generate hypotheses about possible answers to those questions,

    c. thoroughly review all the literature with respect to each question,

    d. revise hypotheses based on research,

    e. carefully state findings and conclusions,

    f. subject all findings and conclusion to peer review and evaluation, preferably including people from all viewpoints.[9]

By following this type of program, people would no longer be taking the easy path of letting others dictate to them. They would no longer need to hide behind fantasies and illusions that, in the short term, may help them temporarily deal with anxieties, fears, and desires, but, in the long-term, will prevent them from establishing a healthier and more balanced outlook on life. There is tremendous personal power and freedom to be gained by undertaking this stance and getting beliefs right.

 PATH TO POWER, ROAD TO RUIN

By following this path, they would take back control of their beliefs, their
destinies, and their lives.

THE TIME
TO CHANGE
IS NOW!

APPENDIX 1

Mass Killing By Ideology

a. Imperialism Killing

Colonial powers used advanced weaponry and military tactics to overpower more primitive peoples in the less developed regions of Asia, Latin America, Africa, and North America. Over two hundred million people were killed in these imperialist programs:

The Mongol Invasions in the 13th century: 40MM
Tamerlane's (Timur) conquests in Asia, 1370-1405: 17MM
Spanish conquests of Central/South America, 16th century: 12MM
The Manchu's Conquest of China, 1600-1644: 25MM
Killing of Native Americans in 17th-19th centuries: 13MM[1]
Leopold's Killing of Congo Natives, (1885-1908): 10MM
Napoleon (1800-1815): 4MM
Imperial Japan and Nazi Germany 1931-1945: 66MM
Russian conquest of North Caucasus, 1817-64: 1.2MM[2]
Shaka Zulu Conquests, 1816-28: 1.5MM
Philippine-American War, 1899-1902, .3MM
French Conquest of Algeria 1830-1962: .8MM
Chinese Conquest of Vietnam (1406-27): .7MM
Gallic War, 58-51BCE, Roman Conquest: 7MM
Italian invasion and conquest of Ethiopia, 1935-41: .8MM
German killing of Herero et al, in SW Africa, 1904-08: .3MM
Alexander the Great. 336-325BCE: .5MM

Revolts against imperial overlords in reaction to decades of exploitation and repression often led to conflicts that were as or more bloody than the original conquests. The leading examples of this phenomenon appear below:

Dungan Revolt, 1862-77: 10MM[3]
Taiping Rebellion, 1850-64: 20MM

Panthay (Hui) Rebellion, 1855-73: 1MM
Dzungar Genocide, 1755-57: .6MM
Mahdi Revolt Against Egyptians/British, 1881-98: 6MM
Expulsion of Germans from Eastern Europe, 1945-7: 2.1MM
Algerian War of Independence from France, 1954-62: .5MM
Mexican War of Independence from Spain, 1810-21: .4MM
Cuban Revolution against Spain, 1895-8: .4MM

b. Communism Killing:

USSR: As many as thirty to forty million people, excluding those lost in the fighting in the Second World War, were murdered in Russia from the time of the Russian Revolution in 1917 to the USSR's collapse in 1989. The major mass killings were precipitated by the communist takeover, the struggle to establish the communists as the dominant power in Russia, the purge of enemies, and the takeover of Afghanistan:

Russian Civil War, Reds vs Whites, 1918-22: 9MM
Stalin's Engineered Ukrainian Famine in early 1930's: 4MM
Stalin's Collectivization Famines in Rest of USSR in 1930's: 3MM
Stalin's Great Purge, 1934-8: 7MM
Soviet-Afghan War, 1979-92: 1.5MM

China: Another sixty million or more people were slaughtered in China from 1925 until 1977 in three distinct phases: First, in the war to establish China as a communist country, then, in the struggle to eliminate all opposition after the communists seized power in 1949, and finally, in various programs to transform and industrialize China and create a successful communist country:

Chinese Communists vs. Nationalists Civil War, 1927-49: 7MM
Purge of regime opponents after takeover,1949ff: 2MM
Mao's Ongoing Purges/Executions, 1949-1969: 9MM
Mao's Great Leap Forward Program in 1959-62: 30MM
Great Proletarian Cultural Revolution, 1966-76: 1MM
Chinese Invasion, Conquest, and Pacification of Tibet, 1950ff.: .4MM

Other Communist Countries: While the USSR and China provided the most dramatic examples of mass killing driven by communism, there were many other countries where there were communist revolutions/

                                    PATH TO POWER, ROAD TO RUIN

conflicts that resulted in the deaths of anywhere from a few hundred thousand to several million people:

North Korean invasion of South. Korea, 1950-3: 3MM
North Korean Repression/Famine, 1949ff.: 3MM
French Indochina War, 1945-54: .4MM
Communist Takeover of Vietnam, 1959-75: 4.2MM
Postwar Vietnam Ideological Purge, 1975-92: .4MM
Cambodian Civil War, 1970-75: .6MM
Pol Pot's Repressive Regime in Cambodia, 1975-79: 1.7MM
Communist Takeover in Ethiopia, 1974-91: 2MM
Angolan Civil War, communist insurgency, 1975-94: .5MM
Mozambique Civil War, communist revolt, 1975-80: .8MM
Communists/Fascists Civil War in Spain, 1936-39: .4MM
Communist Revolution in Greece, 1943-49: .2MM
Guatemalan leftist rebellion, 1960-96: .2MM

c. Racial/Ethnic Killing:

The global slave trade led to the death of millions of Africans during the process of capturing them, transporting them to their final destination, and acclimating them to slavery. In addition, it spawned bloody revolts, and was an important driver of the American Civil War:

Mideast slave trade, 7th to 19th century: 18MM
North Atlantic slave trade, 15th-19th centuries: 16MM
American Civil War, 1860-65: .7MM
Haitian slave revolt, 1791-1803: .4MM

Ethnic/Tribal killing has also taken the lives of millions. The largest mass killings in these areas include:

2nd Congo War, multiple nations, 1996-2003: 4MM
1st and 2nd Sudanese Wars & Darfur 1955-2005: 2.6MM
Rwandan Genocide, 1994: .9MM
Croats genocide of Serbs, 1940-45: .6MM
Tutsi killings of Hutus in Burundi, 1972, 1993: .3MM
Civil War in Yugoslavia, 1992-95: .3MM
Roman Slaughter of Carthage 146 BCE: .2MM
Iraq Anfal, Kurdish Genocide, 1986-9: .2MM

d. Religious Killing

Islam:

Islam has been behind a seemingly unending string of incidents of mass murder during its fifteen-hundred-year history:

Deccan Wars: Muslims vs. Hindus, India, 1658-1707, 4.6MM
Bengali genocide, W. Pakistan in E. Pakistan, 1971: 1.5MM
Armenian Genocide by Muslim Turkey, 1915: 1.0MM
Indonesian Genocide of Communists, 1965-66: .4MM
Iran-Iraq War, 1980-88, .8MM:
Partition of India, Hindus and Sikhs vs. Muslims, 1947: .5MM
Greek Genocide by Muslim Turkey, 1913-22: .3MM
Syrian Civil War, 2011-present: .5MM[4]
Iraq Civil War between Shiites and Sunnis, 2003-07: .2-.7MM
Great Turkish War, Muslims vs. Christians 1682-99: .4MM
Assyrian Genocide by Muslim Turkey: 1914-24, .3MM
Lebanese Civil War—Muslims vs. Christians, 1975-90: .2MM
Indonesian invasion of Christian E. Timor, 1975-99: .2MM

Christianity:

The most significant Christianity-driven mass killings episodes include the following:

Thirty Years War, States and Religions at War, 1618-48, 8MM
French Religious Wars, 1562-98, 3MM
All Christian Crusades, 1095-1291: 3MM
Albigensian Crusade, 1208-29: 1MM
Cromwell's Invasion of Catholic Ireland, 1649-53: .4MM
Spanish Inquisition/ Witch Trials, 16th century: .1MM[5]

Choice of Sources for Mass Killing Incidents

All numerical figures cited above come from Matthew White's *Atrocities: The 100 Deadliest Episodes in Human History* (New York: W.W. Norton 2011).

The process of estimating the number of deaths throughout this book has proven difficult for several reasons. Many of these killings happened in the distant past when accurate death and population records were not kept; some occurred in authoritarian societies that were closed to outsiders who might provide objective reporting on the incidents; and still others took place during wartime when killings occurred behind the lines

  PATH TO POWER, ROAD TO RUIN

and were hidden from public view.

There is also the problem of biases in reporting on either side of the killing. There are those who want to make a political statement about the oppression of the victims and might be inclined to inflate the estimate of deaths to do so. For example, some Hindu groups claim that Muslims killed fifty to eighty million Hindus during their conquests in the Near, Middle, and Far East. While we know that millions were killed, it is difficult to accept the idea that the number is as high as eighty million without more concrete proof.

And there are also biases on the side of the perpetrators who want to deny that the killings ever took place. Turkey denies that the massacre of up to two million Armenians ever happened. The Sudanese Government's disavowed the idea that there was ever a massacre in Darfur, although historians clearly know there was. Some Arabs consistently discredit Israeli claims that there was a Holocaust, in spite of the massive evidence to the contrary.

Because of these issues, historians and other experts have had to make educated guesses based on the information that was available. In the end, however, the most important thing, for the purposes of this book, is to get as good an estimate as possible. To accomplish this objective, I used a consistent methodology about the *order of magnitude* of the numbers, especially relative to other incidents. Precise estimates are generally not available and frankly are not needed to make the point that ideologies can easily lead to mass killing and that mass murders are not rare.

Accordingly, the author chose to use Matthew White's *The 100 Deadliest Episodes in Human History* as the primary source for mass killing data for several reasons. He provides the most comprehensive list of incidents; he uses a consistent methodology to come up with estimates; and he doesn't have an axe to grind for one side or the other.

Other very good books that offer a higher level of scholarship, like R.J. Rummel's, *Death by Government,* and Ben Kiernan's *The Specter of Genocide,* were rejected because they didn't cover as many incidents as White. Still others couldn't be used because they focused on a narrow subset of mass killings, studying a handful of incidents in much greater detail to gain insights into causes. Examples of this group include: *A Century of Genocide, Utopias or Race and Nation,* by Eric D. Weitz, *Century of Genocide, Critical* Essays *and Eyewitness Accounts,* edited by Samuel Totten and William S. Parsons, and *Genocide, A Comprehensive Introduction,* by Adam Jones.

APPENDIX 2

Ideology Definitions

There are a lot of academic arguments about whether belief systems that are called ideologies, like religion or imperialism, are actually ideologies. For example, there are those who argue that religion is not an ideology. Instead, they say it's about the interpretation of scripture, the worship of God, leading a moral life, transcendence, and union with the divine.

However, it is clear that religious belief systems today are about much more than that. In fact, ideologies, such Islam and Christianity, long ago ceased to be solely about these things. These and other religions have, for quite some time, made establishing a position of political power or dominance in their respective societies a top priority. Once they took this step, their beliefs became ideological in character. As Ayatollah Khomeini said during the Iranian Revolution, "Islam is politics or it is nothing."[1]

And also from Khomeini, "In our domestic and foreign policy, we have set as our goal, the worldwide spread of Islam. We wish to cause the corrupt roots of Communism, Zionism, and Capitalism to wither throughout the world. We wish, as does God Almighty, to destroy the systems which are based on these three foundations and to promote the Islamic order of the Prophet..."[2]

Unfortunately, Islam has not been alone in holding and promoting these types of ideas. Evangelical Christianity has also aggressively inserted itself into the United States political system, attempting to push Christian religious beliefs into school curricula, to get important social advances overturned, to push Christianity into all aspects of political life, and to act as an engine to get out the votes and put Christian leaders into public office so the legislative and judicial agenda will mirror their beliefs.

In addition to academic debates about whether religion is an ideology, there are those who argue that imperialism is not an ideology either. For some, imperialism is just about greed and the theft of the resources and possessions of others. Maybe, in pre-industrial times, that was what defined imperialism. We know that there used to be an unending stream of armies from aggressive predatory tribes, plundering their way from Asia into the Middle East and Europe. No sooner had one group taken control than they were replaced by another warrior culture seeking booty and treasure.

Imperialistic adventures were popular in that era, because prior to the industrial revolution, conquest was one of the best ways to grow rich or raise your status in life. It was one of a few scalable opportunities available. The more men you could muster into an army, the more plunder you could take, the richer you could get. Conquest was a business in a time when there were few major economic opportunities; and it was all based on greed and the idea that anyone not of your tribe was dispensable.

For example, the Mongols, who were one of the great imperial nations, were just a highly fragmented steppe people who lived off raiding other tribes, stealing horses, kidnapping women, and taking whatever meager possessions some other group had. It was a difficult life, merely subsistence living. It was also unforgiving. As a woman, if your husband died (as Genghis Kahn's father did), you and your child were cast out from the tribe and left to starve or die. It was only the generosity of some relatives that saved Genghis and his mother.

So, when the Mongols started to coalesce as a power and began moving south from their home in the steppe, they eventually came down to the trade routes and encountered people with much greater wealth than they had ever seen. They definitely wanted to be part of this new reality after living such a marginal existence in Mongolia. So when Genghis Kahn conquered competing Mongol tribes and began merging them into a juggernaut, he was able to become a conquering, booty gathering machine that could not be stopped.

This was imperialism as a business and greed was definitely the motivation. There were no elaborate justifications for the brutality, theft, and mass murder that fueled their advance.

But as we moved into modern times, imperialism did evolve into a full-blown ideology. It became primarily an ideology of justification that rationalized what perpetrators knew then was an illegal and immoral activity, e.g., taking others land and wealth, depriving them of their freedom, and murdering them. The narrative became: we, as a nation with imperialist designs, have the right and duty to extend our influence and control over other regions and populations for several possible reasons: We are better than others; we can develop other nations' resources more fully than they ever could; we can teach them our values, which are better; we can civilize them; or we can convert them to our religion, the one true religion. Imperialists believed that it was their destiny to dominate, to bring less developed peoples the benefits of their civilization, and to transfer their technical knowledge to them in return for access to their lands, their mineral wealth, their markets, and their labor resources.

Today, imperialism has evolved even further. Now it is often driven by multiple ideologies, e.g., nationalism, racism, and militarism, all of which in turn are driven by supremacism. The example of Japanese imperialism in the late nineteenth and early twentieth centuries is instructive of this new reality and really compels us to view imperialism as an ideology.

Japan was imperialistic in that it sought to build an empire that could compete with the leading Western nations, create living space for the overcrowded Japanese homeland, and capture critical raw materials that were lacking in Japan. These goals were backed up by a well-developed and multi-faceted ideology.

Japanese imperialism was racist in its assertion that Japan was the Land of the Gods, that the Emperor of Japan was divine, that the Japanese were the God's chosen people, and that all other peoples were inferior. The Chinese were subhuman. The Koreans were vermin. The Americans were devils. This lowering of other peoples led the Japanese to believe they could exterminate, abuse, and torture inferior others with impunity.

Japanese imperialism was nationalistic in that it sought to establish the Japanese nation as the equal of Western nations. The Japanese felt that they were humiliated as a people because they had to submit to Commodore Perry's demands in 1853, to accept unequal status relative to European Powers in treaties, to give back territory won in the first Sino-Japanese war, and to endure America's severe restrictions on Japanese immigration into the United States. This humiliation weighed heavily on Japan's national identity.

Japanese imperialism was militaristic in that Japan's strategy, beginning in the Meiji Restoration, was to industrialize and build a strong military. A national conscription law was passed, giving the military the ability to indoctrinate all young men who served with nationalistic, racist, and imperialistic propaganda. The military earned tremendous credibility by winning a string of wars in succession—the Sino-Japanese War in 1894, the Russo-Japanese War in 1904, and the Korean-Japanese War in 1905. It annexed Korea in 1910. It invaded Manchuria in 1931 and China in 1937. Then it conquered most of Southeast Asia in 1940-42. As a result, the military in Japan became an independent entity that did not have to answer to the civilian government. It undertook attacks on other countries on its own, assassinated opposition, and was eventually involved in attempted coup d'états.

This blended model of imperialism, as a mix of ideologies, can be found in other places as well in the twentieth century, e.g., in Nazi Germany and Ottoman Turkey. Given this reality, I think it is fair to call imperialism an ideology. In the end, any well-organized set of beliefs or ideas that serves as the basis for developing, implementing, and rationalizing religious, political, and social programs, has to at least be considered as a potential candidate for being called an ideology.

ENDNOTES

Author's Preface
1. White, Matthew, *Atrocities, The 100 Deadliest Episodes in Human History,* New York, W.W. Norton & Company, 2011.

Chapter 1: The Promise of Ideology
1. Putin, Vladimir, *On The Historical Unity of Russians and Ukrainians,* 7/12/22, http://en.kremlin.ru/events/president/news/66181

2. Pewresearch.org., *Modeling the future of religion in America.* How religious composition has changed in recent decades, 9/13/22.

3. Public Religion Research Institute/Brookings survey on Christian Nationalism, *A Christian Nation? Understanding the Threat of Christian Nationalism to American Democracy and Culture,* 2/8/23, https://www.prri.org/research/a-christian-nation-understanding-the-threat-of-christian-nationalism-to-american-democracy-and-culture/

4. Seidel, Andrew L., *The Founding Myth,* 2019, Sterling Publishing New York.

5. Seidel, Andrew L., *The Founding Myth,* Chapter 3, Declaring Independence from Judeo-Christianity, Page 143 (iPhone version).

6. Guthrie Graves-Fitzsimmons; *Christian Nationalism is "Single Biggest Threat" to America's Religious Freedom*; An Interview with Amanda Tyler of the Baptist Joint Committee for Religious Liberty, Center for American Progress, 4/13/22.

7. Jane Mayer, *Dark Money: The Hidden History of the Billionaires Behind The Rise of the Radical Right,* New York, Doubleday, 2016.

Chapter 2: The Problem with Ideology

1. White, Matthew, *Atrocities, The 100 Deadliest Episodes in Human History,* New York, W.W. Norton & Company, 2011.

2. White, Matthew, *Atrocities, The 100 Deadliest Episodes in Human History* Atrocities, Page 554.

3. See Appendix 1a: Imperialistic killing.

4. See Appendix 1b: Communist killing.

5. Merriam-Webster on-line dictionary.

6. White, Matthew, Atrocities, The 100 Deadliest Episodes in Human History, New York, W.W. Norton & Company, 2011, Page 187.

7. https://languages.oup.com/google-dictionary-en/

8. White, Matthew, Atrocities, The 100 Deadliest Episodes in Human History, New York, W.W. Norton & Company, 2012, Pages 80-87 and 161-171.

9. See Appendix 1c: Racial/ethnic killing.

10. See Appendix 1d: Religious killing.

11. Wikipedia, *Ethiopian Civil War,* 400,000-579,000 killed, 1,200,000 deaths from famine.

12. *Worldwide Displacement Hits an All-time High as War and Persecution Increase,* https://-increase/www.unhcr.org/en-us/news/latest/2015/6/558193896/worldwide-displacement-hits-all-time-high-war-persecution-increase.html

13. Eds., Samuel Totten and William S. Parsons, 3rd Edition, *Century of Genocide, Critical Essays and Eyewitness Accounts,* New York, Routledge, 2009, Pages 307-8.

14. White, Matthew, *Atrocities, The 100 Deadliest Episodes in Human*

History, New York, W.W. Norton & Company, 2011, Page 344.

15. White, Matthew, *Atrocities, The 100 Deadliest Episodes in Human History,* Page 400.

16. Wilkerson, Isabella, *Caste, The Origins of our Discontent.* New York, Penguin Random House, 2020, P. 76.

Chapter 3: Ideology Drivers

1. Religion by Country 2024. World Population Review. Retrieved September 24, 2024, from https://worldpopulationreview.com/country-rankings/religion-by-country.

2. Religion by Country 2024. World Population Review. Retrieved September 24, 2024, from https://worldpopulationreview.com/country-rankings/religion-by-country.

3. Lansford, Tom, *Communism,* New York, Cavendish Square Publishing 2008

4. "A theory of human motivation" by Abraham Maslow, Psychological Review. 50 (4): 370–96.

5. Ideological asymmetries in conformity, desire for shared reality, and the spread of misinformation. Jost, et. Al., Science Direct, https://doi.org/10.1016/j.copsyc.2018.01.003)

6. Jost, John; Kay, Aaron; Thorisdottir, Hulda, The Social and Psychological Bases of Ideology and System Justification, New York, Oxford University Press, 2009, Page 213.

Chapter 4: Utopianism--Heaven Can Wait

1. Eds., Claeys, G., Sargent, L. T., *The Utopia Reader,* New York, New York University Press, 1999, Pages 12-13.

2. Eds., Claeys, G., Sargent, L. T., *The Utopia Reader*, Page 71-6.

3. King James Bible, *The New Indexed Bible*, John A. Dickson Publishing Co., Chicago, Illinois, 1923, Genesis, Chapter 2, Verses 8-10, 19, 22.

4. Eds., Claeys, G., Sargent, L. T, *Utopia Reader*, II Baruch, 73:1-74:2; Pages 67-68.

5. King James Bible, *The New Indexed Bible*, John A. Dickson Publishing Co., Chicago, Illinois, 1923, Apocalypse of John 7:15-17.

6. King James Bible, Apocalypse of John 21:1-4.

7. *The Koran* 55:41, Pages 56-7. Dawood, N.J., Translator, Penguin Books, NY NY, 1974.

8. Eds., Claeys, G., Sargent, L. T., *Utopia Reader*, Chapters 18, 19, 20.

9. Ed. R.C. Tucker, *The Marx and Engels Reader*, 2nd Edition, New York, NY, W.W. Norton & Company, 1978, Page 490.

10. Ed. R.C. Tucker, *The Marx and Engels Reader,* Page 490-1.

Chapter 5: Absolutism--The Refuge of Small Minds

1. https://languages.oup.com/google-dictionary-en/

2. Abi-Habib, Maria; *Christians, in an Epochal Shift, Are Leaving the Middle East,* Wall Street Journal, 5/12/2017.

3. Repucci, Sarah, & Slipowitz, Amy; *Freedom House Report, Freedom in the World 2022,* 02/2022, Page 4.

4. Jost, John et al. *The Social and Psychological Bases of Ideology and System Justification*, New York, Oxford University Press, 2009, Page 187.

5. Stern, Jessica, *Terror in the Name of God, Why Religious Militants Kill,* New York: Harper Collins Publishers, 2003, Page 69.

6. Krakauer, Jon, *Under The Banner of Heaven,* 2003, Doubleday, Pages 72 and then 31.

7. Burton, Dr. Robert, *On Being Certain, Believing You Are Right Even

When You Are Not. New York, St. Martin's Griffin, 2008, Page xiii.

8. Burton, Dr. Robert, *The Certainty Bias: A Potentially Dangerous Mental Flaw,* Scientific American, 10/9/08; https://www.scientificamerican.com/article/the-certainty-bias/

9. Mill, John Stuart, *On Liberty.* Mineola, NY, Dover Publications Inc., 2002, Page 15

10. Sagan, Carl, *The Demon Haunted World: Science as a Candle in the Dark.* Ballantine Books, Random House, 2011.

11. Rovelli, Carlo, *Anaximander and the Birth of Science.* Kindle Edition, New York, Riverhead Books, the Penguin Group, 2023.

12. Feynman, Richard, from the lecture, given at the Galileo Symposium in Italy, 1964: *What is and What Should be the Role of Scientific Culture in Modern Society?.*

13. Mack, Burton. *Who Wrote The New Testament, the Making of Christian Myth.* New York, NY: Harper Collins Publishers, 1995, Page 5.

14. Ehrman, Bart D. *Jesus Interrupted, Revealing the Hidden Contradictions in the Bible (and Why We Don't Know About Them.)* New York: Harper One, Harper Collins Publishers, 2009, Page 183.

15. Ehrman, Bart D. *Misquoting Jesus, The Story Behind Who Changed the Bible and Why.* Pages 87-9, New York: Harper Collins San Francisco, Harper Collins Publishers, 2005.

16. Burr, W.H., *Self-Contradictions of the Bible,* New York, BiblioBazaar, 2007.

17. Kahneman, Daniel, *Thinking Fast and Slow;* New York: Farrar, Straus, and Giroux, 2011, Page 4.

18. Harris, Sam. *The Moral Landscape.* New York, Free Press, Simon & Schuster, 2010. Pages 102-3.

19. Haidt, Jonathan, *The Righteous Mind*, New York: Pantheon Books, 2012, Page 46.

20. Haidt, Jonathan *The Righteous Mind*, Page 47.

21. Haidt, Jonathan, *The Righteous Mind*, Page 54.

22. Newberg, Dr. Andrew, and Waldman, Mark R.. *Born to Believe, God, Science and the Origin of Extraordinary Beliefs*. New York: Free Press, 2007.

23. Newberg, Dr. Andrew, and Waldman, Mark R., *Born to Believe, God, Science and the Origin of Extraordinary Beliefs, Page xix.*

24. Newberg, Dr. Andrew, and Waldman, Mark R., *Born to Believe, God, Science and the Origin of Extraordinary Beliefs,* Page 253.

25. Newberg, Dr. Andrew, and Waldman, Mark R.. *Born to Believe, God, Science and the Origin of Extraordinary Beliefs,* Page 9.

26. Haidt, Jonathan, *The Righteous Mind*, New York: Pantheon Books, 2012, Page 47.

27. Newberg, Dr. Andrew, and Waldman, Mark R., *Born to Believe, God, Science and the Origin of Extraordinary Beliefs,* Pages xvii-xviii.

Chapter 6: Supremacism--Raising Ourselves and Lowering Others

1. King James Bible, *The New Indexed Bible*, John A. Dickson Publishing Co., Chicago, Illinois, 1923, Genesis, Chapter 1, verse 26.

2. King James Bible, Genesis, Chapter 12, verse 2.

3. King James Bible, Deuteronomy 7:6.

4. King James Bible, Galatians 3:28-9.

5. Quran 5:3."Today I have made your religion complete for you, and I have completed My blessing upon you. I have accepted that Islam will be your religion..." While all Scriptures come from God and carry the same Message, the scope of Scripture varies. The Qur'an's scope is comprehensive, covering every circumstance (18:54) for its

post-globalist recipients. It indicates completion; no further Divine Scripture will come afterward. Prior Scriptures were subject to tampering, whereas the Qur'an has been given Divine protection(15:9).

6. Waller, James, *Becoming Evil*, 2nd Edition, Oxford, Oxford University Press, 2007, P. 183.

7. Wilkerson, Isabella, *Caste, The Origins of our Discontent*. New York, Penguin Random House 2020, P. 70.

8. Demick, Barbara. *Nothing to Envy, Ordinary Lives in North Korea*. New York: Spiegel & Grau, Penguin Random House, 2015, Pages 27-28.

9. Demick, Barbara. *Nothing to Envy, Ordinary Lives in North Korea*. New York: Spiegel & Grau, Penguin Random House, 2015, Pages 27-28.

10. Singer, Peter. *Marx, A Very Short Introduction*. New York: Oxford University Press, 1996. Page 49.

11. https://www.splcenter.org/fighting-hate/extremist-files/ideology/male-supremacy

12. Lindner, Evelin. *Making Enemies, Humiliation and International Conflict*. Westport, CT: Praeger Security International, 2006, Page 8.

13. Sternberg, Robert J., *In Search of the Human Mind*, Fort Worth, Texas, Harcourt Brace College Publishers, 1995, Page 453, Table 13.2, referencing work by James Marcia.

14. Waller, James, *Becoming Evil*, 2nd Edition, Oxford, Oxford University Press, 2007, Page 177.

15. Edsall, Thomas, *The Resentment that Never Sleeps*. New York Times, December 9, 2020.

16. Sapolsky, Robert M., *Behave, The Biology of Humans At Our Best and Worst*. New York: Penguin Books, Penguin Random House, 2017,

Pages 392-3.

17. Waller, James, *Becoming Evil*, 2nd Edition, Oxford, Oxford University Press, 2007, Page 174.

18. Waller, James, *Becoming Evil*, Page 174.

19. Waller, James, *Becoming Evil*, Pages 174-5.

20. Waller, James, *Becoming Evil*, Page 175.

21. Rediker, Marcus. *The Slave Ship, A Human History*, New York, The Penguin Group, 2008, Page 328.

Chapter 7: Three Dangerous Ideas Currently in Play

1. Silver, Laura & Fetterolf, Janell, Who Likes Authoritarianism and How Do They Want to Change their Government, Pew Research, 02/28/2024 https://www.pewresearch.org/short-reads/2024/02/28/who-likes-authoritarianism-and-how-do-they-want-to-change-their-government/

2. Rummel, R.J., *Democracy, Power, Genocide, and Mass Murder*, from the March 1995 Issue of the Journal of Conflict Resolution, Pages 3-26).

3. Sha, Wenbiao, *The Political Aspects of Land Appropriation in China*, Journal of Development Economics, Volume 160, 01/2023, https://www.sciencedirect.com/science/article/abs/pii/S0304387822001274

4. Solzhenitsyn, Aleksandr I, *The Gulag Archipelago, 1918-1956, An Experiment in Literary Investigation I-II*, New York, Harper & Row, Publishers, 197.

5. Kwame Anthony Appia, *Race in the Modern World-the Problem of the Color Line*. Foreign Affairs, March/April 2015.

Chapter 8: The Road to a Better Future

1. Lester, Greg, *Why Bad Beliefs Don't Die*, Skeptical Inquirer, Volume 24.6, November/December 2000.

2. Pewresearch.org., *Modeling the future of religion in America.* How

religious composition has changed in recent decades, 9/13/22.

3. Smith, Jean, *The Beginner's Guide to Walking the Buddha's Eightfold Path,* New York, Bell Tower, 2001.

4. Council of Secular Humanism https://www.google.com/searc h?client=safari&rls=en&q=council+on+secular+humanism&i e=UTF-8&oe=UTF-8#vhid=zephyr:0&vssid=atritem-https:// secularhumanism.org/

5. Lewis, Michael, *The Big Short,* New York, W.W. Norton and Co., 2011.

6. Lewis, Michael, *Moneyball,* New York, W.W. Norton and Co., 2003.

7. Arquilla, John, *Bitskreig, the New Challenge of Cyberwarfare,* Cambridge, England, Polity Press, 2021 , Page 73/4, Kindle Edition.

8. Knaus et al., *Where's the Evidence?,* Free Inquiry, December'07/ January'08, Pp 38-43.

9. Lett, James, *A Field Guide to Critical Thinking,* Skeptical Inquirer, Winter 1990.

Appendix 1: Mass Killing by Ideology

1. Rummel, R.J., *Death by Government,* New Brunswick, NJ, Transaction Publishers, 1994, Page 70.

2. Wikipedia, Russian Conquest of the North Caucasus, 1817-64.

3. Bender, Jeremy & Macias, Amanda, *5 of the 10 Deadliest Wars Began in China,* Business Insider, 10/06/14, Dungan Revolt.

4. Wikipedia, *Syrian Civil War,* Page 1.

5. Wikipedia, *Witch Trials & Spanish Inquisition.*

Appendix 2: Discussion of Ideology Definitions
1. Bernard Lewis, *Islamic Revolution, The New York Times Book Review,* 1/21/88.

2. Islamic Government, *Islam and Revolution, Declarations of Imam Khomeini,* 1981, P. 91.

 PATH TO POWER, ROAD TO RUIN

BIBLIOGRAPHY

Almond, G.A., Appleby, R.S., and Sivan E.. *Strong Religion, the Rise of Fundamentalisms Around the World.* Chicago: University of Chicago Press, 2003.

Applebaum, Anne. *Gulag, A History.* New York: Doubleday, a Division of Random House, Inc., 2003.

Arendt, Hannah, *The Origins of Totalitarianism.* New York: A Harvest Book, Harcourt Brace, and Co. 1948.

Armstrong, Karen. *The Battle For God, A History of Fundamentalism.* New York: Ballantine Books, Random House, 2001.

Armstrong, Karen. *Buddha.* A Lipper Viking Book, Penguin Group, Penguin Publishing, 2001.

Armstrong, Karen. *A History of God, The 4000 Year Quest of Judaism, Christianity, and Islam.* New York: Ballantine Books, Random House, 1993.

Arquilla, John, *Bitskreig, The New Challenge of Cyberwarfare.* Medford, MA, Polity Press, 2021.

Avalos, Hector. *The End of Biblical Studies.* Amherst NY: Prometheus Books, 2007.

Barash, David P.. *Revolutionary Biology, The New Gene Centered View of Life.* New Brunswick, NJ: Transaction Publishers, 2001.

Balkanian, Peter, *The Burning Tigris, the Armenian Genocide and America's Response.* New York: HarperCollins Publishers, 2020.

Becker, Ernest, *Denial of Death.* New York: Free Press Paperbacks, 1973.

Bell, Rudolph. *Holy Anorexia.* Chicago: The University Chicago 1987.

Boyer, Pascal, *Religion Explained.* New York: Basic Books, Perseus Books, 2007.

Ben-Ghiat, Ruth, *Strongmen, Mussolini to the Present.* New York, W.W. Norton & Company, 2020.

Berreby, David, *Us and Them, The Science of Identity.* Chicago, University of Chicago Press, 2005.

Berlin, Isaiah, *The Crooked Timber of Humanity.* Princeton: Princeton University Press, 1990.

Bloom, Howard, *The Lucifer Principle, A Scientific Expedition into the Forces of History.* New York, The Atlantic Monthly Press, 1995.

Bratlinger, Patrick. *Dark Vanishings, Discourse on the Extinction of Primitive Races, 1800-1930.* Ithaca, NY: Cornell University Press, 2003.

Burr, W.H., *Self-Contradictions of the Bible.* New York, BiblioBazaar, 2007

Burton, Richard, *On Being Certain, Believing You Are Right Even When You Are Not.* New York: St. Martin's Griffin, 2008.

Chang, Iris, *The Rape of Nanking.* New York: Penguin Books, 1998.

Chandler, David, *Voices from S-21, Terror and History in Pol Pot's Secret Prison.* Berkeley: University of California Press, 1999.

Chirot, Daniel, *Modern Tyrants*. Princeton: Princeton University Press, 1994.

Claeys, G. and Sargent, L.T., Eds. *The Utopia Reader*. NewYork, NYU Press, 1999.

Dawkins, Richard, *The God Delusion*. New York: Houghton Mifflin, 2006.

Dawkins, Richard, *The Selfish Gene*. New York: Oxford University Press, 1989.

Dawood, N.J., Translator, *The Koran*. Penguin Books, NY NY, 1974.

De Las Casas, Bartolome, *A Brief Account of the Destruction of the Indies*. BN Publishing, 2008.

Demick, Barbara, *Nothing to Envy, Ordinary Lives in North Korea*. New York: Spiegel & Grau, Penguin Random House, 2015.

Dikotter, Frank. *Mao's Great Famine, the History of China's most Devastating Catastrophe, 1958-62*. New York: Walker & Company, 2011.

Dolot, Miron, *Execution by Hunger*. New York: W.W. Norton, 1987.

Efron, E. J., *Real Jews, Secular vs. Orthodox and the Struggle for Jewish Identity in Israel*. New York: Basic Books, Perseus Books Group, 2003.

Ehrman, Bart D., *Jesus Interrupted, Revealing the Hidden Contradictions in the Bible (and Why We Don't Know About Them.)* New York: Harper One, Harper Collins Publishers, 2009.

Ehrman, Bart D., *Misquoting Jesus, The Story Behind Who Changed the Bible and Why*. New York: Harper Collins San Francisco, Harper Collins Publishers, 2005.

Ellens, J. Harold, Ed., *The Destructive Power of Religion, Violence in Judaism, Christianity, and Islam*. Westport CT: Praeger Publishers, 2007.

Fitzgerald, Frances. *The Evangelicals, the Struggle to Shape America*. New York: Simon and Schuster, 2017.

Freeden, Michael, *Ideology, A Very Short Introduction*. New York: Oxford University Press, 2003.

Frankl, Victor E. *Man's Search For Meaning*. Boston: Beacon Press, 2006.

Friedman, Richard Elliott, *The Hidden Face of God*. New York: Harper Collins San Francisco, Harper Collins Publishers, 1995.

Freud, Sigmund, *The Future of an Illusion*. Mansfield Center, CT, Martino Publishing, 2011.

Gallagher, Winnifred, *Spiritual Genius, The Master of Life's Meaning*. New York: Random House, Inc., 2001.

Gellately, R. and Kiernan, B., Eds. *The Specter of Genocide, Mass Murder in Historical Perspective*. New York, Cambridge University Press, 2003.

Goldhagen, Daniel J. *Worse Than War, Genocide, Eliminationism, and the Ongoing Assault on Humanity*. New York: Public Affairs, a member of the Perseus Books Group, 2009.

Gourevitch, Philip, *We Wish to Inform you that Tomorrow, We Will Be Killed With Our Families, Stories from Rwanda*. New York: Picador, Farrar, Straus, and Giroux, 1998.

Gray, John. *Black Mass, Apocalyptic Religion and the Death of Utopia*. New York, New York: Picador, Farmer, Straus, and Giroux, 1998.

Griffith, James L., *Religion that Harms, Religion that Heals, A Guide for Clinical Practice*. New York: The Guilford Press, 2010.

Hadot, Pierre. Chase, Michael trans. *What is Ancient Philosophy?* Cambridge: The Belknap Press of the Harvard University Press, 2002.

Haidt, Jonathan, *The Righteous Mind*. New York: Pantheon Books, 2012.

Harris, Sam, *The End of Faith, Religion, Terror and the Future of Reason*. New York: W.W. Norton & Co., 2005.

Harris, Sam. *The Moral Landscape*. New York, Free Press, Simon & Schuster, 2010.

Hayek, F.A., *The Road to Serfdom*. Chicago: The University of Chicago Press, 1994.

Hedges, Chris, *American Fascists, The Christian Right and the War on America*. New York, Free Press, 2006.

Hitchens, Christopher. *God is not Great. How Religion Poisons Everything*. New York: Twelve, Hachette Group USA, 2007.

Hitchens, Christopher. *Letters to a Young Contrarian*. New York, Basic Books, Perseus Book Group, 2005.

Hoffer, Eric, *The True Believers, Thoughts on the Nature of Mass Movements*. New York: Harper Perennial Modern Classics, Harper Collins Publishers, 2002.

Hofstede, Geert, *Cultures and Organizations: Software of the Mind, Intercultural Cooperation and Its Importance for Survival;* New York: McGraw Hill, 1991..

Hood, Ralph. W. Jr., Hill, Peter C. and Williamson, W. P., *The Psychology of Religious Fundamentalism*. New York: The Guilford Press, 2005.

Hochschild, Adam. *King Leopold's Ghost, A Story of Greed, Terror, and Heroism in Colonial Africa*. New York: A Mariner Book, Houghton Mifflin Company, 1999.

Jones, Adam, *Genocide, A Comprehensive Introduction*, 2nd Ed. London: Routledge, Taylor and Francis Group, 2011.

Jost, John T., Aaron, C.K., and Thorisdottir, H, Eds., *The Social and*

Psychological Bases of Ideology and System Justification. New York: Oxford University Press, 2009.

Kahneman, Daniel, *Thinking, Fast and Slow*. New York: Farrar, Straus, and Giroux, 2011.

Kaku, Michio, *Parallel Worlds, A Journey Through Creation, Higher Dimensions, and the Future of the Cosmos*. New York: Doubleday, Random House, 2005.

Kershaw, Ian. *Hitler, 1889-1936 Hubris*. New York: W.W. Norton & Co., 1998.

Kiernan, Ben, *Blood and Soil, A World History of Genocide and Extermination, from Sparta to Darfur*. New Haven: Yale University Press, 2007.

Kiernan, Ben, *The Pol Pot Regime, Race, Power, and Genocide in Cambodia Under the Khmer Rouge, 1975-9*. 3rd ed.. New Haven, Yale University Press, 2008.

Kimball, Charles, When Religion Becomes Evil, Five Warning Signs. New York: Harper Collins San Francisco, Harper Collins Publishers, 2003.

King James Bible, *The New Indexed Bible*, John A. Dickson Publishing Co., Chicago, Illinois, 1923.

Krakauer, Jon, *Under the Banner of Heaven, A Story of Violent Faith*. New York: Doubleday, A Division of Random House, 2003.

Lester, Gregory W., *Why Bad Beliefs Don't Die*. Skeptical Enquirer.org. Skeptical Inquirer Magazine, Volume 24.6, November/December 2000

Levine, George, Ed., *The Joy of Secularism, 11 Essays for How We Live Now*. Princeton: Princeton University Press, 2011.

Lewis, Michael, *Moneyball*. W.W. Norton and Co., NY, NY, 2003.

Lewis, Michael, *The Big Short, Behind the Doomsday Machine*. New York, W.W. Norton & Co. 2010.

Lindner, Evelin, *Making Enemies, Humiliation and International Conflict*. Westport, CT: Praeger Security International, 2006.

Maalouf, Amin, trans. Barbara Bray, *In the Name of Identity, Violence and the Need to Belong*. New York: Arcade Publishing, 2000.

Mack, Burton, *Who Wrote The New Testament, the Making of Christian Myth*. New York, NY: Harper Collins Publishers, 1995.

Martin E Marty and R Scott Appleby, eds., *Fundamentalisms Observed, a Study of The Fundamentalism Project* conducted by the American Academy of Arts and Sciences. Chicago, The University of Chicago Press, 1991.

Mascaro, Juan, Translator. *Bhagavad Gita*. London: Penguin Books, 1965.

Mascaro, Juan, Translator. *The Upanishads*. London: Penguin Books, 1965.

McRaney, David, *How Minds Change, the Surprising Science of Belief, Opinion, And Persuasion,* One World Publications, 2023.

Moore, B.N. and Parker, Richard, *Critical Thinking*, 7th E . Boston: The McGraw Hill Companies, 2004.

Newberg, Andrew, and Waldman, Mark R., *Born to Believe, God, Science and the Origin of Extraordinary Beliefs*. New York: Free Press, 2007.

Newberg, Andrew; D'Aquili, Eugene; & Rause, Vince, *Why God Won't Go Away*. New York: Ballantine Books, Random House Publishing Group, 2002.

Oliver, A.M. and Steinberg, Paul, *The Road to Martyr's Square, A Journey into the World of the Suicide Bomber*. New York: Oxford University Press, 2005.

Orwell, George, *Animal Farm*. New York: Plume Publishing, Penguin Group, 2003.

Orwell, George, *1984*. New York: Plume Publishing, Penguin Group, Harcourt Brace, 1949.

Pagels, Elaine, *The Gnostic Gospels*. New York: Random House, 1979.

Pagels, Elaine, *The Origin of Satan*. New York: Vintage Books, Random House, 1995.

Paine, S.C.M., *The Japanese Empire, Grand Strategy from the Meji Restoration to the Pacific War*. Cambridge, England: Cambridge University Press, 2017.

Passmore, Kevin. *Fascism, A Very Short Introduction*, New York: Oxford University Press, 1996.

Perez, Joseph, and trans. J Cook, *The Spanish Inquisition, A History*. New Haven: Yale University Press, 2005.

Pinker, Steven, *The Better Angels of our Nature, Why Violence Has Declined*. New York: Viking Penguin, The Penguin Group, 2011.

Popper, Karl R., *The Open Society and Its Enemies, Volume 1, the Spell of Plato*. Princeton, Princeton University Press, 1971.

Popper, Karl, *The Poverty of Historicism*. London: Routledge Classics, 2002.

Prunier, Gerard, *Darfur, A 21st Century Genocide*, 3rd Ed.. Ithaca: Cornell University Press, 2008.

Radzinsky, Edvard, *Stalin*. New York: Anchor Books, Random House, 1997.

Rediker, Marcus, *The Slave Ship, A Human History*. New York, Penguin Books, The Penguin Group, 2007.

Rieke, R.D., Sillars, M.D., and Peterson, T.R.. *Argumentation and Critical*

Decision Making, 7th ed.. Boston: Pearson, 2009.

Rothstein, Edward; Muschamp, Herbert; and Marty, Martin E., *Visions of Utopia.* New York: Oxford University Press, 2003.

Rudin, Rabbi James. *The Baptizing of America, The Religious Right's Plans for the Rest of Us.* New York: Thunder's Mouth Press, 2006.

Rummel, R.J. *Death by Government.* New Brunswick, NJ, Transaction Publishers, 1994.

Russell, Bertrand, *Why I Am Not a Christian.* New York: A Touchstone Book, Published by Simon and Schuster, Inc., 1957.

Sageman. Marc, *Understanding Terror Networks.* Philadelphia: University of Pennsylvania Press, 2004.

Sapolsky, Robert M., *Behave, The Biology of Humans At Our Best and Worst.* New York: Penguin Books, Penguin Random House, 2017.

Seidel, Andrew L., *The Founding Myth, Why Christian Nationalism is Un-American.* New York Sterling Publishing, 2019.

Plokhy, Serhii, *Lost Kingdom, The Quest for Empire and the Making of the Russian Nation.* New York, Basic Books, 2017.

Service, Robert, *Lenin, A Biography.* Cambridge: The Belknap Press of Harvard University Press, 2000.

Shaw, Martin, *War and Genocide, Organized Killing in Modern Society.* Cambridge UK: Polity Press, 2003.

Shermer, Michael, *The Believing Brain, How We Construct Beliefs, and Reinforce Them as Truths.* New York: Times Books, Henry Holt & Co., 2011.

Shermer Michael, *How We Believe, Science, Skepticism, and the Search for God.* New York: Owl Books, Henry Holt & Co., 2003.
Smith, Homer, *Man and His Gods.* New York: Grosset's Universal

Library, Grosset and Dunlap, 1952

Smith, Huston, *Why Religion Matters*. New York: Harper Collins San Francisco, Harper Collins Publishers, 2001.

Smith, Jean, *The Beginner's Guide to Walking the Buddha's Eightfold Path*, New York, Bell Tower, 2001

Smith, Shawn, *The User's Guide to the Human Mind, Why Our Brains Make Us Anxious and Neurotic and What We Can Do About It*. Oakland CA: New Harbinger Publications, Inc., 2011.

Snyder, Timothy. *Bloodlands, Europe between Hitler and Stalin*. New York: Basics Books, Perseus Books Group, 2010.

Solzhenitsyn, Alexsandr, *The Gulag Archipelago, An Experiment in Literary Investigation*, 1918-56. New York: Harper & Row Publishers, 1973.

Stearns, Jason K., *Dancing in the Glory of Monsters, the Collapse of the Congo and the Great War of Africa*. New York: Public Affairs, 2012.

Stenger, V. J., *God, the Failed Hypothesis, How Science Shows That God Does Not Exist*. Amherst, NY: Prometheus Books, 2007.

Stern, Jessica, *Terror in the Name of God, Why Religious Militants Kill*. New York: HarperCollins Publishers, 2003.

Storr, Anthony, *Feet of Clay, Saints, Sinners, and Madmen, a Study of Gurus*. New York: Free Press Paperbacks, Simon and Schuster, Inc. 1997.

Totten, Samuel, and Parsons, William S., *Century of Genocide, Critical Essays and Eyewitness Accounts*, 3rd Ed. New York: Routledge, Taylor and Francis Group, 2009.

Tsunetomo, Yamamoto, Translator, Mukoh, Takao, *The Hagakure, A Code to the Way of the Samurai*. Tokyo: The Hokuseido Press, 1980.

Tucker, Robert C., Editor, *The Marx-Engels Reader,* 2nd Edition. New York: W.W. Norton, 1978.

Versus, Arthur, *The New Inquisition, Heretic Hunting and the Intellectual Origins of Modern Totalitarianism*. New York: Oxford University Press, 2006.

Waller, James, *Becoming Evil, How Ordinary People Commit Genocide and Mass Killing*, 2nd Edition. New York: Oxford University Press, 2002, 2007.

Ward, Jonathan, *China's Vision of Victory*. Atlas Publishing and Media Company, 2019.

Weatherford, Jack, *Genghis Kahn and the Making of the Modern World*. New York; Three Rivers Press, Crown Publishing, Random House, 2004.

Weitz, Eric, D. Genocide, *Utopias of Race and Nation*. Princeton: Princeton University Press, 2003.

White, Matthew. *Atrocities, The 100 Deadliest Episodes in Human History*. New York: W.W. Norton & Co., 2013.

Wilkerson, Isabella, *Caste, The Origins of our Discontent*. New York, Penguin Random House 2020.

Zuckerman, Phil, *Society Without God*. New York: New York University Press, 2008